The Slugs of *Tackett's Mill*

Kerry Young

PAGE PUBLISHING, INC.
New York, NY

First originally published by Page Publishing, Inc. 2018

ISBN 978-1-64350-187-1 (Paperback)
ISBN 978-1-64350-189-5 (Digital)

Printed in the United States of America

PROLOGUE

November 1990

It may prove to be of some interest to Americans across the country to gain some insight into the complexities of living near the nation's capital. Every day, over three hundred thousand people commute from the suburbs of Washington, DC, to their jobs in the District or in Northern Virginia. The resulting traffic congestion is typical of any large city. The commuting methodology is not.

To alleviate traffic, High-Occupancy Vehicle (HOV) lanes are designated (HOV-3 for a total of three in the car, the driver picks up two slugs) to encourage commuters to leave their cars, ride with someone else, and gain the advantage of a less heavily traveled road. The natural economics of the situation have caused many of the suburbs to have parking areas, designated (Park n' Rides) and non-designated, enabling drivers to become riders before reaching the main thoroughfares. Designated pickup points have gained wide acceptance for drivers needing riders. The return ride home in the afternoon is from designated pickup points—for instance, the Pentagon, back to the rider's point of origin.

The benefits of this arrangement are mutual. The cost of living in this area is very high. Slugging prevents wear and tear on the car and paying parking fees. It also eliminates (well, reduces) the stress of bumper-to-bumper traffic for the slug. For the driver, picking up a slug entitles use of the segregated HOV lanes at Springfield, ten miles from DC (in 1990). Typically, regular traffic will be bumper to bumper compared to HOV's 55+ mph. The savings in commute time and expense can be considerable. Because the driver needs only two people, just being there is the only requirement so that these people have become known as slugs. Slugging is the process of parking your car, standing in line, and riding to work with a total stranger. Other cities might have a crime problem with this arrangement, but Washington has the world's largest office pool in the Pentagon—government and contractor employees all with the same problem of getting to work efficiently. All with offices to commute to and mortgages to pay.

One such slugging arrangement is at Tackett's Mill, Lakeridge, Virginia, which is twenty-five miles south of DC. These commuters rely on Interstate 95 (I-95) for getting to work. I-95 has the reputation (and deservedly so!) of being the most continually congested highway on the east coast. It stretches from Florida to Maine like a vital artery, with few alternatives. It is not unusual for it to be congested for other than rush-hour reasons.

The regular I-95 traffic lanes are always (bank on it!) slow during rush hour through the Dale City, Woodbridge, area. The HOV lanes rules are widely disregarded as police feel pulling someone over for not having a rider slows traffic and is dangerous for the officer. The Virginia Railway Express (VRE), use of an existing train system, was to help too, but no change has been noted, despite the train ridership increasing steadily. It was touted to take an entire lane of traffic off I-95. Who are these people that ride the train yet make no difference in I-95 traffic? Former van poolers? New housing farther south that can now commute in comfort?

The latest wisdom and funding was to extend segregated HOV lanes to Quantico, eight miles south of Woodbridge. The five-year construction plan to accomplish this is being completed at this writing.

I quickly learned after moving into the area in 1985 that leaving for work earlier was better, as heavier traffic also meant more accidents. It wasn't unusual for the thirty-minute commute to take in excess of one and a half hours due to an accident. In some instances (snow, crime, major accident), the normal half-hour commute can take over six hours.

But the fact that people stand in line in the dark and get into a stranger's car in perfect safety is a demonstration of supply and demand at its finest. No contracts, no fees, no discussion, just an orchestrated ballet of efficiency.

This is a diary of one of these slug pickup sites. This microcosm of society shows the mind-set of the worker bees in our nation's capital as they arrive at work. The game is played out with regularity. The players become familiar yet nameless characters. They are "The Slugs of Tackett's Mill.

While I began slugging in 1985, during this period, starting in 1990, I was driving a compact car, a Toyota Starlet, which was not slug friendly, being too small and having only two doors. It should be noted that time and dates are in military format—the twenty-four-hour clock and day, month, year.

Wednesday, 28 November 1990

Unusually balmy morning. I picked up two portly civilian men, both wearing sweaters. (Why is it the older guys have bellies sticking out?) Anyway, I tried starting a conversation after a long, awkward silence. I took the shortcut, Occoquan to Devil's Reach roads, commenting as I did so, "A lot of people taking this shortcut now." To which the guy in the front seat commented pessimistically there would be a long line on Devil's Reach. Other than that, the front seat civilian would only grunt at my comments.

"Traffic is easy if they are slow or hit the light by the KFC [restaurant]."

"Mmm!" (Grunt.)

"Everybody's having trouble getting off the on-ramp."

"Mmm!" (Grunt.)

"At last the HOV is working the way it should!" To which the back seat civilian commented he saw a sign saying HOV would revert to HOV-4 come January (1991).

I told them they should lessen the requirement and be like California (with HOV-2). "Problem is no one is running this show. Several months it's four, then three, then four again. Who's controlling this change?"

Back seater said, "Van poolers, most likely!"

Front seater said, "Mmm!" (Grunt.)

As HOV-only access was gained, a large blue van shot past as I reached 65 mph (55 mph speed limit). Shortly after, a highway patrol car activated his lights as we pulled even. He continued to accelerate and pulled over the blue van. We discussed radar detectors being illegal in Virginia, but if you had one, you wouldn't be caught speeding. Back seater stated, "Police are experimenting with laser detectors."

I commented, "They needed the ESM (Electronic Surveillance Measures) gear the military had." I dropped them off at the Pentagon and proceeded to park in nearby Crystal City, where I worked.

Monday, 3 December 1990

A cool morning, lots of cars picking up slugs, including me. As two cars ahead loaded, a civilian came back and got in the back seat. After we pulled up, an Air Force colonel got in front for our third occupant. His knees were at the dashboard, and I bumped his leg in shifting and turning the radio volume down. Civilian was very talkative: Washington Redskins beating Miami 42–20, Giants at 49ers tonight, HOV I-95 vs. HOV I-66. The latter was a lengthy comparison with 95 having more accidents but a better HOV lane. I-66 had no HOV requirements until the beltway. The colonel said little. Nothing, actually, until I asked if either had heard that the Iraqis fired some missiles over the weekend. The colonel stated it was to test their own indigenous missile capability since the Soviets were no longer selling them Scuds. Probably a sign the embargo was working.

Wednesday, 5 December 1990

The water pump was replaced on Tuesday. Oil leaked from the timing belt. On a cold, blustery morning, an Air Force lieutenant colonel got in back, and as nearly as I could tell, a woman got in front. She mentioned it was cold, especially with wet hair, and I replied she might want to change that policy. We in the front seats chatted all the way in about Toyotas and their reliability. She asked specifically what kind of Toyota it was, not in the "because I never want to ride in one again" vein but out of an interest in liking it. I explained the nine-year-old car had over 108,000 miles and when the repair bills met the car payments I would get rid of it. She said she had a Camry, and yes, it was reliable but only five years old. I tried to coax the lieutenant colonel into the conversation once, on the topic of where we work, but it seemed to be a bother for him and interrupted his shut-eye period. So I resigned myself to the front-seat conversation. She was new to the area, two weeks, although it later came out she had only moved from closer in and working across the river (Potomac) at the Treasury building in Crystal City. She worked seven to four but occasionally worked credit hours. We discussed the new homeward-bound HOV only to Springfield and problems in getting to and from work. She was quite different from the usual two silent life-forms that accompanied me to work.

Wednesday, 9 January 1991

No school (a University of Colorado master's class at the Pentagon) tonight but am supposed to go to a meeting at IBM, Manassas, at 1300. I picked up a civilian (front seat) and lieutenant colonel in the Air Force in the back seat. As always, front seat patron refused to part with his briefcase even at the expense of the rear seat occupant's leg room. Said he was afraid he would forget it. Forget it? It was all he had. Anyway, they were congenial, and we talked traffic and Persian Gulf all the way to work. No major traffic problems.

Trip to Manassas was cancelled in favor of a meeting in contracts. Picked up two slugs for the trip home at the Pentagon, an Air Force major and lieutenant colonel in back. They immediately established a rapport that lasted the entire trip home. It was as though I didn't exist. Seems the lieutenant colonel was the Air Force reserve coordinating officer for Desert Shield. Major, a goofy guy with glasses, threw out how it was better to be a C-141 pilot than a C-5 pilot but that there was a shortage of C-5 pilots. "Because," the lieutenant colonel commented, "of all the crews on crew rest at once. Used 'em up like so much snot locker tissue. They are just too critical to operations overseas." Some reservists (doctors, lawyers, airline pilots) are complaining (he was responsible for responding to

Congressional inquiries, a big job) they are losing too much money. The major took a stand on this. "By God, they knew that when they signed up, have to take the good with the bad, had no sympathy for them." Lieutenant commander continued that others made out, augmenting current duties with reservist volunteer flights.

Monday, 14 January 1991

Very cold. Garage door stuck halfway up, enough to get out. Air Force Major got in back and scrambled to behind me until I said we weren't taking three people. Civilian guy got in front. Both extremely grateful to get in out of the cold. Discussed pro football and where the winners would play (Raiders to NY Giants, Buffalo to 49ers) and whether we would be at war by Wednesday. Civilian said he would attack a day early to catch the Iraqis off guard. Major said public opinion wouldn't allow that.

Wednesday, 16 January 1991

Tuned in the radio before eating my oatmeal to see if we went to war with Iraq. No change. It felt a lot like trying to catch the score of a late baseball or football game from the previous day.

In the steady downpour of cold rain, I found two eager slugs with a third willing to come. From the little I saw of the woman, who turned out to be a financial analyst for the Army, was headed for the Pentagon. As we drove off, I could see the eagle of a Navy captain or Air Force colonel.

We began discussing the war situation and in particular how it affected our everyday lives. By the increase in security. The Pentagon had three bomb scares yesterday, they said.

As we negotiated the egress from Lakeridge and the I-95 on ramp, the discussion between the (it turned out) Air Force colonel and financial analyst evolved to the bombings and scares during European duty in '84 to '86. Both remembered them, then realized they both were there in Germany at the same time. While an Army analyst, the woman was married to an Air Force officer. While they continued their tryst, I struggled with defogging the windshield as the haze crept lower and lower.

The colonel was Japanese-American. He asked what I did, so I explained being a retired Navy officer, now a beltway bandit. He said it was his experience contractors generally didn't come to work early. But he rationalized most people coming from the service are type A. And even after taking less responsible jobs, like his friend Joe, eventually gravitate to the same accomplishment level. Joe was in landscaping.

He then got into what he would like to do on retirement, which was train dogs. Labs for guide dogs. And then he described how to do it in great detail.

Wednesday, 23 January 1991

Extremely, bitterly cold in the teens. The garage door has developed the characteristic of working sluggishly in the cold. Not opening all the way. Or not closing all the way. This morning, it stopped halfway open. I ran it open manually, engaged the latch, and closed it automatically. It kept bouncing back up, so I stopped it six inches off the ground and returned my attention to the bucking Toyota Starlet. With the choke in the second detent, I still needed to rev the engine to keep it from dying.

I entered the main street, Old Bridge, between masses of traffic but soon became part of one at a stop light.

The slug line was twenty or so people long. A minivan loaded in front of us as a very big Hawaiian-looking man looked at the back seat I offered. Then we let a small older woman get in back, and he sat in front, occupying all the space the right seat had to offer.

The big (not fat, just tall and proportionate) man expressed amazement at the car, asking what kind it was. I recognized this (after he rejected the back seat and struggled with his belongings and the seat belt) to be a case of the "what kind of car is it so as to never get caught in one again" syndrome. I told him it was an '81 Toyota Starlet, which probably confirmed his suspicions.

The woman grew quiet in back after our initial discussion of how cold it was. The man stated he was always cold here, being from Hawaii. He asked me if I worked at the Pentagon. I told him, no, but gave up asking for Crystal City riders that I was retired Navy.

Being a good, congenial slug despite the conditions, he said I didn't look more than thirty-five (I was forty-six). I related going to Navy flight school directly out of college, and he said, well, being fat in the face often signifies an older man. He asked if I ran. Striking a nerve bundle of intense interest, I explained four miles during weekdays and eight on weekends. He said he wanted to run more but had no rec facility. I explained Dale City rec center and the new Lakeridge elementary school with a track were nearby. He said he would go to it.

Told him I was driving due to school after work. He asked what school course. I explained taking University of Denver master's classes in the Pentagon. He said he was a computer analyst, hoping to get a transfer in government work to Hawaii. We discussed various software programs and how dumb some customers were. Completed the drive in about thirty-five minutes, dropping them off in good shape.

Thursday, 24 January 1991

CNN news reported Iraqi Scud missiles were successfully intercepted heading for Tel Aviv, Israel. And the garage door didn't stick going up or coming down.

The slug line was extremely long. Pulled up behind another loading car, and two young women got in. A bouffant-haired one in back and a slim black woman in front. I tried to get the black woman to put her hanger bag of clothes under the hatchback compartment, but true to slug form, she felt it was fine even if it inconvenienced the back-seat occupant. She didn't object though. I'm going to have to investigate to see if the slug psyche believes an abyss to exist aft of the rear seat.

Anyway, the black woman turned and began a conversation with the young bouffant-haired woman in back that didn't stop until the Pentagon. It was mostly me listening to them, although I interjected when possible to remind them I was in the car.

A comparison of the services started, the black woman being Army and the white woman Army and Navy. I explained about being Navy retired, and the front seat enjoined with getting hit and then drowning as opposed to Army just getting hit (in combat). I observed, "How often are we at war? Living conditions in your service should prevail—mud for Army versus air conditioning for Navy or Air Force." Back seat added that Air Force has better living conditions overall. We all agreed.

Seems the two were good friends. Both had two kids; back seater, a single parent. Talked responsibility, kids crying at a store and their discipline. Both related irresponsible men they had to associate with. Front seater was going to a class on computers with a lot of smart-aleck people. Dropped them at the Pentagon south entrance.

Tuesday, 29 January 1991

Class was switched from Monday to Tuesday night, probably so the instructor could recover from late Sunday night revelry from the Super Bowl (Giants 20, Bills 19). Not very cold, in the forties.

Picked up a Japanese-looking man and what turned out to be his wife. Right off, we realized they had ridden with me before. "I remember you. You're the retiree from the Navy. And this is an '81 Toyota Starlet." To which I replied, "I remember you. You're the one with the dogs and want to be a vet." No, wrong guy. His wife dropped out of the conversation after she laughed with us at my remembering incapacity.

We talked all the way in. About cars—he thought Toyotas were great maintenance wise. He wanted to buy a new car but friends had been in accidents soon after buying one. I told him they weren't built for collisions the way they should and that air bags and four doors were important.

We got into raising kids and discipline. His father used a belt, and his mom would leave the discipline to him.

Arrived at the Pentagon drop-off at 0630.

Wednesday, 30 January 1991

Close to fifty degrees. Long wait to enter traffic at Old Bridge and very heavy to the Tackett's Mill slug line. Short, stubby woman— half American, I would guess—debated with a very tall Air Force captain who would take back seat. Logic won, and the short, squat elderly woman got it. Naturally, the captain had a suit bag and suit-case. He alone barely fit, and I was mortified that, for the first time, I would not be able to get someone in the car and reject him for size. He managed to get in, with gear, knees against the dashboard, brief-case under his legs, suit bag on them. I persuaded him to let the suit bag go to the back seat. He couldn't be persuaded to put anything in that dreaded space; his fear of leaving it was so great.

Neither spoke all the way in. I switched to CNN radio news, and we listened to the border clashes, Iraqi aircraft flying to Iran, and a transport coming back. Bush's State of the War was quoted.

On a couple of occasions, I tried to stimulate conversation, but the captain just grunted. Or said "Yeah!" We had a super easy com-mute, arriving at the Pentagon at 0620.

Monday, 4 February 1991

Normal routine, no glitches to the slug line. In the forties but expected to reach seventy degrees today. Long, long slug line. Arrived at 0555 and pulled up to the head of the line, threw open the door, and announced, "Pentagon!"

Two officers, the first was the tallest in line. *Just my luck*, I thought. He hesitated, then reluctantly got in. The one getting in back got in "all at once" as if to emphasize the smallness of the cramped, constrained confines he was resigned to. It was an unwritten rule that slugs are taken in order, regardless of size or any other consideration. I know he was an officer whose rank I couldn't determine, but likely lower than the colonel who sat in front as he deferred to.

As a reflection of their reluctance to get in, I said, "Just your luck to get a small car!" To which they both eagerly responded, "No, we're just glad to get a car. Besides, the price is right, so we can't complain."

After this, the officer in the back didn't speak. As a matter of fact, the colonel in front didn't either. Until I mentioned I would get a four-door car for slugs when this one quit. Trouble is it hasn't. "Why should you?" he responded.

Discussed Jordan throwing in with the alliance because Saddam wasn't leaving Kuwait. He said Queen Nor and he would be overthrown as a result, living in DC. I had switched from pop rock WASH-FM to CNN radio news. A Huey, a Cobra (helicopters), and a B-52 had crashed. Also, we had misled our own Marines; seven of eleven killed. Arrived at 0620, Pentagon, south entrance.

Wednesday, 6 February 1991

Light drizzle, still unusually warm (yesterday reached seventy degrees). Probably in high forties, low fifties. Chili Day at work. Several people brought crock pots full of chili to simmer all day until lunch when it goes on sale, with condiments, sour cream, crackers, cheese, etc. Problem was in securing the crock pot on the aft part of the car so as not to interfere in the back seat for my rider. I used 90 mph speed tape to secure the heater base to the lid and tape to secure it all to the car. I was certain everything behind the back seat, in the black hole, would be chili covered. This was a large crock pot.

The slug line was in transition when I pulled up. Two cars loading. Probably a Land Rover in front of a few people in line but individuals streaming to the line. Only a loading wait. Maybe due to the drizzle.

Anyway, a woman came forward and got in back when I flung open the door and called, "Pentagon!" A tall Air Force captain (equivalent to a Navy lieutenant) slowly, reluctantly, disgustedly sat in front. They all wanted BMW or Rolls Royce comforts.

I mentioned how short the line was. They responded briefly, and that was the last thing either said until they got out at the metro bus drop off at the Pentagon. A coworker had shown me a news article the previous day the Air Force was taking over three-fifths of the Pentagon. No wonder I keep getting them.

Commute was without incident until approaching Occoquan Road. I slid right on Old Bridge to turn. Moments later a large van, impatient with the Old Bridge line, suddenly turned out in front of us with no warning. I initially didn't think I could stop in time, and the captain threw up his hands to brace for impact. We didn't hit, and the van almost immediately swerved back to the left back into the line. I expressed my concern for the chili's status, and we continued in. Often the van pool drivers act as though they own the road and have precedence over all other traffic. After all, they have more passengers than individual slug cars do.

Monday, 11 February 1991

After a nice weekend, today has suddenly turned colder, in the thirties with 15–20 mph winds. Long slug line. Picked up a short woman and a really tall guy. Both civilians. Got the young man in front to open up a little on the Sugar Ray Leonard fight. He mentioned George Foreman coming back because he had to feed his family of five. All offspring named George. I mentioned I thought that would lead to confusion. But he said George didn't seem to mind. Just call George to dinner. Said I was glad I wasn't a female in his house. The woman, middle-aged or younger, only thanked me as she got out.

Wednesday, 13 February 1991

Very cold, expecting rain or possibly snow today. Long slug line. Two cars loading in front of me but an older Russian hatted man eagerly came to the car and climbed in back. An Air Force officer with one bar that didn't shine hesitantly got in front. Very tall with a nylon book bag in his lap. The officer and I discussed the war in the Gulf briefly. Two missiles had hit a bunker killing four hundred women and children. Forty charred bodies had been recovered (do Iraqis multiply by ten?) A Russian envoy was told by Saddam he was ready to talk but only about an overall peace, linking Palestinians and not mentioning leaving Kuwait. No change. Then the car grew silent as I negotiated the stops and starts of I-95. I had hit almost every red light in leaving Lakeridge. Now it was the usual slowdowns, at the on-ramp, approaching Ft. Belvoir and near Springfield (where HOV land construction slowed traffic). When our conversation died, I switched from pop music to CNN news with Gordon Graham (soundtrack to TV). Besides the radio and the car noises, the only sound was the old man in the back coughing and clearing his throat. At one point in the HOV-only lanes past Springfield, we passed a van with a loud *whop, whop* noise. Or was it us? I continually hoped the car wouldn't break down but fully expected it to happen sometime. After all, we were over 110,000 miles now. Not much by many accounts, but the most I had ever had.

I glanced up and saw two lights from a low-flying helicopter, followed by a traffic report on the radio that fit his position nicely. I said that must have been the reporting helo. To which the officer said he thought it was the van next to us, although it sounded like an H-1 helicopter, being familiar with the sound they make. Reminded me of the Ready Room at NAS Whiting Field during Navy helicopter flight training. There was an air conditioner that made the H-1 sound identically! As though by recording. It was always bizarre waiting for a training flight, hearing the continuous *whop, whop, whop* without a helo nearby.

Wednesday, 20 February 1991

Sixty-five degrees! Spring-like morning, short slug line. Two cars loading, pulled up and got an Air Force major for the back seat, Army major front seat. The Army major and I talked Soviet peace proposal, with CNN news background, all the way in. Air Force major in back participated in adding mostly brief repetitions of the front-seat conversation. Or short mumblings. We considered alternatives should the US accept the plan, Saddam disposition, reparations to Kuwait (Iraq has no money, so why ask?), leave then with some self-defense to keep aggressive nations out. Then we got heavily into reserve participation. The Army major mentioned lawyers and doctors suing because they weren't retired on time and were ordered to the Persian Gulf.

Monday, 25 February 1991

Temperature probably in the high thirties. No delay on pickup, two Army officers. A lieutenant colonel in front, I think. Thought I caught a glimpse of the silver oak leaf. Actually, the Army uniform is peculiar that way. With no jacket, they have do-dads all over their dark-green uniform. Wearing a black jacket and holding their hat, they are one indistinguishable person.

I started with music. Down near Hechinger's (hardware store), a bus cut through our line of traffic to the next lane, leaving, I thought, a gap. Somehow it was filled without traffic ahead moving. It caused me to stop rather abruptly, causing some concern, I sensed, from my slugs. I switched to CNN News and cranked up a war discussion. Until we got to the on-ramp and traffic was not merging well or smoothly at all. I worked as quickly as I could to the far left lane, which would become the HOV lane over the next hill. As we crept near, a single driver cut in front and stayed there. When the HOV signs were passed, I showed my brights. Again, in a few seconds. I mentioned my disgust. My front-seat slug pointed out it wasn't 0600 yet when HOV started but actually 0555. So he was legal, damn!

While in the HOV-only lanes, separated from the regular traffic by Jersey barriers, we noticed a single driver pass us. We thought him nervy and wondered where the cops were. We soon found out. Near the Navy Annex, one had pulled a speeding car pool car over. The single driver had won a daring gambit!

Monday, 4 March 1991

War ended during the break in classes. I haven't had to drive alone yet as this class is directed study, and I haven't been directed yet. Returned to my old car pool.

Bob drove his full-sized black van with hundreds of thousands of miles. There are only three seats, though a van-sized platform covers the back. All three seats are sheepskin covered and rock in their mounts. So we picked up a slug. It was drizzling, but only one person, an Air Force colonel, stood in the slug line. As he got in, a peculiar odor, like black sen-sens, wafted up. Must have been some kind of aftershave. Whatever it was, was odorific, and I couldn't wait until he debarked at the Pentagon. Gary Smith rode home to prevent any reoccurrence.

Wednesday, 6 March 1991

Car pool broke down. My turn to drive. Picked up Bob. Had to wait a moment at the empty slug line. Weather was pleasant, still dark around 0600. Picked up an officer of some sort, and I asked him to sit behind me as Bob used all the space available on his side. Tried to start a conversation with the back-seat slug, but he never said anything, except thanks, when he got out. Had a red and gray gym bag but refused the offer to stash it in the "black hole" behind the back seat. Bob and I chatted all the way in.

Wednesday, 20 March 1991

Had to drive to get our daughter's orthodontic records, molds, and X-rays. Picked up an enlisted Air Force woman (couldn't make out rank at a glance), and a well-dressed civilian guy got in the back. Slug line was long on a pleasant morning. Talked how remarkable slug arrangement was all the way in. Guy in back even contributed occasionally. She had relatives coming in, she said, and they didn't believe (it was her second week) one could stand in line and catch a ride with total strangers.

Thursday, 21 March 1991

Car pool broke down, again. Coming home, driving the van. With just two of us, I get to pull up to the doubled-up slug line at the Pentagon, needing only one rider with four or five seats available. So we volunteer four seats, although I'm sure the added weight costs in fuel economy. Two older women got in back and two Air Force officers just behind us. The officers talked shop all the way home, sounding like they were trying to impress the rest of us, who were forced to listen.

Friday, 22 March 1991

I was a rider in our car pool today, Larry's Nissan. We needed riders going home and got two. I was reading *Augustine's Laws* for class and occasionally quoted an anecdote to which the older woman slug would chuckle and comment. We also had an Army officer in back.

Wednesday, 3 April 1991

Car pool broke down again. Friday was pre-Easter rush, one and a half hours to home. Bob drove Friday, Monday, and Tuesday in his big black van with the lambskin-covered seats and the jump seat that is not fastened completely. Monday I had soccer practice (coached our son's team) at 1830. With traffic backed up from an earlier accident, suddenly Steve wanted to go to Thrifty car rental, out of the way, back on Route 1.

Cold out, long slug line. Van and car ahead. I called, "Crystal City!" as I rolled forward. No response. An old gray-haired guy climbed in back. He couldn't bend. An Army colonel was in front.

I started talking about the time change, and the old guy commented on the sun in his eyes, a good reason for the time change. New York plates, Chevy Caprice, new, with two passengers paced us all the way in. One of the two passengers smelled of pipe tobacco, probably the old guy in back.

Friday, 5 April 1991

No one showed up for car pool. We had been out late going to the Cherry Blossoms at the Tidal Basin and eating out, so I didn't call when I got home. Result? No riders. I picked up two slugs after waiting in the car line for five minutes. Air Force Major in back— eagerly climbed in out of a light, cold drizzle—and a gray-haired guy in front. After some discussion of alternate routes out of Lakeridge, nothing more was said. Older guy breathed heavy, and I glanced at him several times to see if he was awake. He was alert, just breathing heavy.

Monday, 8 April 1991

Yesterday Tom, the sixth member of our car pool, called. He needed a ride in but would be out going home. The rest of the pool was on travel—two on world travel, England and Greece, and I thought, *Okay, just a slug stop. At least it's on the way.* Now I had to back-track for one guy and pick up a slug. Didn't seem fair.

Picked up an Air Force major, tall guy, with two carry-on items. He acted as though he were standing up in back. Struggled to get in but was congenial enough. Most discussion was between Tom and me about sales of houses—two of four sold near him. His Syracuse and submarine work. Weather was very, very nice. Cool but warming to eighties.

Wednesday, 10 April 1991

Larrie Cable, part of the Westridge car pool, couldn't drive as he had his van torn apart. I was really looking forward to the break in driving duties. We picked up an Army major that sat upright, with his eyes closed, causing me to look several times to see if he was looking out or listening to our conversation.

Thursday, 11 April 1991

Drove in early to take computer in. Just drove straight in on HOV before it started. Beat the 0600 HOV start time by ten minutes.

Coming home in really nice weather, I picked up an Air Force woman but didn't catch her rank. Had glasses, dark hair, fairly short. She listened to a tape all the way home. Only heard click approaching Tackett's Mill as she turned it off. After dropping her off, Larrie observed a Datsun 240 following me to my house. Stopped at the end of the driveway; our slug had left her "brains" (notebook) in the back seat. *Lucky to see me again*, I thought.

Monday, 15 April 1991

No call from the car pool. I'm tired of making all the connections and wondering if someone will show up at 0600. Jumped in the car at 0545 to drive to Tackett's Mill car-pool lot. Light, cold misty rain. Brought running gear bag with collapsible umbrella. Long slug line in the dark. All of us lined up, facing the street, as though we were there for selection. We waited with some anticipation for what we would get on our turn. A Plymouth Voyager took two of us. I mentioned having one and what year was this; '90 was the reply. He pointed out the heating control to my left. It was wonderful after the cold, wet camping weekend I had experienced at Andrew's Air Force base to gain certification as a camping Cub Scout leader. I drifted into the slug posture of comatose for the trip. The van was quiet except for the driver's CD of classical music. Crystal clear. So clear I found myself listening for the scratches until I drifted off. I came to as we rounded the bend for the Pentagon off-ramp. I think your body knows the whole composite trip as a series of swaying a certain amount, as though the body recognized our location regardless of the lack of visual support. The cool mist was okay to walk in as I made my way to Crystal Park 2. I only had to walk from the Pentagon to the start of the Crystal City Underground shops to gain cover from the rain.

Slugged going home, short line. Got into a Buick Regal with plush seats and headrests. I sat behind the driver, who had seat all the way back and inclined back. Had to sit legs spread for the seat back. Read class project material all the way home. Woman in right seat (his wife) talked incessantly but barely audible over rear speaker. She had a large sharp nose and stopped talking only long enough to primp in her mirror several times. I don't believe the driver said a word all the way. Air Force major to my right looked out the whole time.

Tuesday, 16 April 1991

Weather turning nice going in. Car pool still in disarray. Slug line was fifty or more long, and I was tempted to go back to the car and pick up riders. Heard good stories while waiting though. Woman pulled up to the mailbox near the line, and three guys got in. She was surprised as she was only mailing letters!

Going home. A woman and two guys got in a car with me at the Pentagon for Tackett's Mill. When the driver got in the slow lane for the Springfield off-ramp, they suggested switching lanes. He said, "Why? We're getting off at Springfield anyway!" He said he asked for riders to Springfield, not Tackett's Mill! Woman said she was not getting out of the car, so he drove to Woodbridge, another ten miles for all of us. Next time he'll make it clear for his sake.

Thursday, 25 April 1991

Car pool broke down—five guys, none in. Beautiful morning, four cars ahead for slugs, no line. Land Rover, high seats, in front appeared to have one passenger, waiting for one more. An Air Force guy headed for it, and a woman was next from the right. I was sure I would get her, but instead, the Rover needed two, and she got in ahead of me. Next was an Air Force major who cheerfully jumped in back, and an older woman with glasses and a sweater reluctantly got in front.

Traffic was normally heavy, and I took the cut-off at Occoquan and hit the light to Route 123 just right, no hesitation. Just after crossing the I-95 overpass, a car whipped around our left, trying to cut in at the on-ramp. Or at least looking for the opening that's usually there as cars make the entry turn. Except this morning, the van in front of us had two cars packed close ahead. The deviant car had no chance but to wait as the van, and then we passed. It was a young black guy who just shrugged as I glared and shook my head at him. I was hugging the van's rear to keep him out. Meanwhile, the schizoid timid woman on my right had her arms up on the dash and was mumbling something about "We're going to crash. Let him in, crazy driver!" To which I at first took to mean the other guy was crazy, watch out for him. But she continued with her mumbling tirade, saying, "I don't want to be in an accident. I know he was wrong, but it's not worth an accident." Which irritated me to the nth degree. I loaded my repertory cannon but restrained myself from firing. I wanted to tell her there would be no accident, I was in control, and while our car was ten years old, I wasn't about to scratch it now. I said those guys need to be arrested and taught a lesson. She replied, "We're not the police, though." I restrained myself again, considering my options. I could tell her off and make the next thirty to forty minutes unbearable. Or/and she could be my slug again sometime. I decided to play the incident down, and nothing more was said, although she sat there, I sensed, very tensely, with arms folded. A glance later revealed she had her eyes closed. The Air Force major was shut-eyed too. I guess if you can't see what's happening, it won't.

Highlight of the commute was the HOV lanes at Springfield were extended, allowing us to enter HOV sooner.

Tuesday, 14 May 1991

Had to call car pool to cancel both ways. Classmate never called back from answering machine message. Car didn't start after six to seven tries. Finally, it did. Medium line, nice morning. An Army colonel, woman, blonde, cropped hair, got in back. Tall guy like Joe DiMaggio got in front. He gave up his briefcase to the back seat. She slept in back; he read the paper and looked out.

Monday, 14 June 1991

0600, sunny morning. Lot almost full, about fortieth in line! Went quickly, and an Air Force colonel picked up five of us as I reached the head of the line. Heavy, heavy traffic. Dodge LE van played 107.3 MIX radio. No accidents but took about forty-five minutes. After being dropped off, walking by Doubletree Hotel, there were three new bright-red tri-state tour buses. Two potbellied drivers out front of one of the buses. One said to the other, "Yowee, here we are in Washington, DC, land of the queer and druggy!"

Going home. No line! Fifteen or so for Potomac Mills. This was a streamline day. I caught an elevator going down, no line. There was an Isuzu with a young woman driving and a close-cropped guy on the right with a Marine haircut. Her Marine cap was in the back. Although she had shorts and a blouse, she looked a lot like a man. The Marine had to get out to let me in. The non-directional music resounded off my right ear; the speaker was mounted. I dozed, no air conditioning, comfortable with the windows down. We passed a small car with the rear bashed in. Emergency vehicles, rubbernecking, slow down.

Tuesday, 15 June 1991

Going in two older women talked about plumber problems all the way in.

Going home. I was on a hot, humid Dale City bus to the Pentagon, and as we approached, the bus filled with smoke. Light rain forced all the smoke under the new bus canopy the Pentagon had erected. I was in front and easily got out in time, but the rest surely inhaled smoke before getting off. I was in the slug line, behind twenty slugs. Craig and John (friends) pulled up in John's Honda, and I took Craig's invitation, out of slug line turn, joking they would kill me for short-circuiting the line. Air conditioning was good, but Craig reviewed Candelas "kicking me out of the car pool." An Air Force guy on my right was indifferent to our discussions. I dozed the remainder of the trip, no music. Accident at King Street expedited our run, retarding public traffic.

Wednesday, 16 June 1991

Nice weather at 0600. Forty slugs in line moving fast. Got one of the last four parking spots. Air Force officer and I got a new Honda Civic. Or rather a three-hundred-plus pound man with a car wrapped around him. Surprisingly, I had leg room, moved up, and the Air Force officer said he was roomy too. The driver, a ponderous young guy was similar to Jabba the Hut in girth. Wore a short sleeve shirt and tie, had glasses, played 107.3 MIX FM radio. He lane-jumped and had the annoying habit of clasping his hands and resting them on his ample gut when decelerating. Traffic was congested at the bottom of the hill approaching the Pentagon, and he made little attempt to get me a safe drop-off spot. He stopped traffic at the intersection to let me out obnoxiously.

Friday, 6 August 1991

Rain, rain, rain. Got Sargent (Sarge) going home, look for previous write-up. All routes accident delayed.

Monday, 9 August 1991

My brother, Glen, is flying into town. Long, long slug line. Where were they Friday? Lined up next to an old guy who kept fidgeting with earphones and radio / tape player in a bag under his shoulder. After numerous cars picked up and the line moved across from the McDonald's lot, a Ford Astro van asked for Crystal City. Not normally asked since most slugs work at the Pentagon or State Department. Young long-haired driver with glasses. One guy in shotgun, and then belatedly, a guy wanted in after I was about to close the door. He ran conversation briefly, then we had the radio Charlie Casserly, Redskin Report. Dropped off at the northern end of Crystal City at the Route 1 overpass.

Going home. Twelfth or so in line. Dark storm-like weather to the north of DC, but just hot and humid here. White Suburban station wagon. Air Force captain driving and Marine captain in the right seat. A little Buddha in an ornamental, clear capsule hung from the rearview mirror, as well as a string of something like little corn husks or firecrackers. And a bag of potpourri. News on the radio was of the Redskins-Browns game. For the first time in remembered history, it was blocked out in the greater DC area. The driver complained tickets cost $35, just for a preseason game, and the area was slimy. Rather see it at home. Traffic was heavy. Again, I read country magazine and dozed. The civilian on my right read a pocketbook.

Whenever relatives wonder how we can slug to work with strangers when we could get the serial chainsaw killer for a driver we just have to point out this is a unique situation. Where everyone is commuting to DC to sit at a computer and then commute back again. Everyone going to work to earn the mortgage and car payment. Never in over twenty-two years of slugging did I hear of any—none—cases of abduction or intentional mistreatment. We were all in this together doing the same routine.

Tuesday, 10 August 1991

Parked in front of McDonald's drive-through window in the parking lot. Early line to second but soon grew to corner by 0600. Saw the white Suburban with Buddha. An Air Force officer (I couldn't see his rank) took three after I made a fool of myself leaping for a minivan. They took two with room for four. The Nissan Ultima was discussed by me (behind the driver) and the driver. He had popped the trunk for my suit bag and queried where I was going. "Atlanta," I replied, but first, a day's work. After work, I walked over to Reagan Airport for a TWA flight to Atlanta.

Days Inn driver was thin and slightly stooped with dark tousled hair not ready to give his age away. His skin was the aged, wrinkled skin of an older person, and his face showed experience and travel, belying his hair's testimony to youth. His left eye was "not right." He either had an artificial eye or lost muscle control of it as it didn't dilate or move to focus. His drawl punctuated his Southerness. We began our final trip from the Days Inn to Rockwell (about five minutes away), discussing how kids didn't know their geography. We had to know states, capitals, countries, and continents. Kids these days were automatically passed to the next grade. Geography and a sense of direction were essential. He related how his wife could read a map but couldn't find her way after a circle around the mall. His dad couldn't read or write but taught him direction skills. He taught his thirty-year-old boy twins how to survive by taking them five miles away at seven years old and dropping them off with matches, string, and a bag of rock candy. His wife fretted, and he finally had to go get them, but they were happy and snug. He mentioned a scout leader that lost two kids in a freak snow storm. He died, but the kids found a cabin and broke in. I mentioned the guy who cut his legs off with a pocket knife after becoming stuck in a national park out west, and he recalled the Andes survivors, the soccer team as I remember it, that ate their dead to survive. He had chased a rat around after being parachuted into the French Alps during the war. Even now, he carries matches and string. The string to tie off your pants and fill them with leaves. He was never successful at rubbing sticks to start a fire, so he carried matches. His black coffee slapped in his styrofoam cup.

Monday, 24 September 1991

Air Force colonel got in back, long legs. Front guy went back with the seat. As we got underway, the colonel wanted to know what kind of car this was, as if needing to know where to assess blame and avoid this type of car forevermore. Later, when quietly drowsing along in traffic, he could be heard snoring in heavy sleep.

Wednesday, 26 September 1991

Two guys in business suits got in. Both polite in adjusting the seat. One in front recorded HOV violation to report and went to

Crystal City, just like me. Highway patrol/police have the policy of not stopping cars for violations, but you could call in, and when there were a number of complaints, they would contract the car owner to warn them of an impending ticket. Very toothless and it was widely ignored, so that the valid HOV users were punished instead of the violators.

Monday, 28 September 1991

All three Army guys discussed digging for foxholes (word for trenches), water in Hawaii. Back Army colonel and guys in front had seen each other before, likely at cities in Germany they had been stationed at.

Tuesday, 29 September 1991

New Jeep Cherokee, Army colonel driver, Navy captain front right, Air Force colonel right back, next to me. Classical music, worked for Keefer, worked for UN, one year in Israel, and one year in Jordan.

Wednesday, 30 September 1991

To Bethesda Naval Hospital for daughter Megan's cardiology.

Thursday, 1 October 1991

Air Force sergeant, small car (VW rabbit), two packs of Marlboros on the dash. Asked about his parking pass at the Pentagon. He was in a car pool but now at the Navy Yard for inauguration committee. (Navy was moving from Crystal City to the Navy Yard.)

Friday, 2 October 1991

Going home, I caught *big* rundown Cadillac Brougham. Radio cut in and out, car creaked and groaned like it was falling apart. Gray-haired and bearded driver with older gray-haired woman said he needed to work on it to get mileage above 9 mpg.

Monday, 5 October 1991

Morning saw a pickup ram an Astro van head-on. Truck turned from far right lane to left. Long slug line saw it. Big white Cadillac picked me up. He had replaced brakes, been to Harper's Ferry. Picked up a woman at Hechinger's (local hardware store) at the intersection of Old Bridge Road and Route 1, just before getting into HOV.

Tuesday, 6 October 1991

At Bethesda Naval Hospital for Megan (our daughter).

Wednesday, 7 October 1991

Civilian driver in a Plymouth. Two Air Force majors, one with coffee mug, talked with the driver about Ross Perot's half-hour economics talk.

Tuesday, 13 October 1991, day after Columbus Day Holiday

Air Force major in back. Gray-bearded guy smelled of pipe or body odor? Played classical music on WMAL all the way in. Driver drove stiff armed, going to Crystal Mall, no discussion. He was stone silent the whole trip until I announced the need to be dropped at the bottom of the off ramp hill to the Pentagon.

Wednesday, 14 October 1991

Drove and parked along no-parking street. Entrance open but station wagon took the spot. In the afternoon, tow trucks were in the area.

Thursday, 15 October 1991

Had to drive to IBM, Manassas, for helicopter trainer meeting.

Friday, 16 October 1991

"Assisted" slug line in getting three per car. Some reluctant. Big car, Air Force guy on the right, sleeping, breathing quietly. Guy in the front right, casually dressed, snored loudly. Driver changed radio channels to wake him up; head went forward, and he continued to snore.

Going home at 1530, second in line! Sporty car with two young women took one with two seats available. Next car was Buick Regal with a black woman driver, with another black woman in the shotgun seat. She was playing black women singing music and moved the speaker to the front, likely to accommodate me. I could tell they were disappointed, uncomfortable with picking me up (as was I). I buried myself in the paper until arrival at McDonald's parking lot at Tackett's Mill. Except for two occasions: when the right lane driver drifted in front of us, and when a deer was running northbound in the center of traffic, tongue hanging out.

Monday, 19 October 1991

Volvo with a big Air Force major driver. A small white-haired lieutenant in the right seat had the back all the way reclined. He asked if I needed him to move, but I declined, trying to be nice, but won't next time. I sat spread-eagled, unable to move. They talked slow and low. Traffic tied up at the 14th Street Bridge due to protesters protesting violence in DC and the death penalty. I-270 is blocked by a flaming tractor trailer up and halfway around the beltway.

Thursday, 22 October 1991

Missed breakfast doing algebra with one of our kids. Long line, went quick. New car, roomy, behind blonde "aura" hair. Driver had on a flannel shirt. Calm guy but took an aggressive shortcut. He kept being positive, with an eager driving attitude. Front two talked a little and laughed. Guy on left, civilian, was stone rigid and still. HOV congested due to rubbernecking southbound accident. Top of one car ripped off. Only police and tow truck were left at the scene. There was silence in the car as we all looked in wonder. Same feeling as ship fire at night at sea. Just observing a disaster, wondering what caused it, what it did to people on board. Car was Isuzu Stylus, must be Isuzu's premiere car of the line.

I listened to popular music until halfway there, then switched to WMZQ. The radio lamented, "I cried as she died, but they walked on by."

Going home. Steve of old car pool intercepted me in the Pentagon parking lot. I thought he was going to hit me until I recognized him. Didn't talk all the way home.

Friday, 23 October 1991

Cold, about forty degrees in line. Marines (by haircut) picked me up in a newish jeep-like vehicle. Both in civvies. Service personnel frequently carry or stage their pressed uniform at work and wear civilian clothes to work so as not to wrinkle them. Driver said, "Damn, I forgot to say 'Happy Birthday!' to my wife. I did order flowers, she'll know I couldn't have ordered them this morning." Guy in right seat scarcely moved or spoke. Like a supreme leader, the driver asked to leave work early. "Sir!" Driver liked trunk bumper sticker. "Gun Control, ignorance in action!" Listened to WMZQ radio.

Monday, 26 October 1991

Going in a van (an XE caravan), I took five slugs. If there are many slugs and few cars, this is acceptable so the slugs do not have to wait. If there were more cars waiting, taking the minimum number of slugs is the unwritten rule so each car could get riders. The van's speaker was in my ear; the driver played Grease Man, a sleazy radio talk show host that specialized in speaking grossly. I would be embarrassed to let anyone think I listened to his trash talk.

Tuesday, 27 October 1991

Oldsmobile Calais. We discussed Voyagers/Caravans at length. No radio all the way in. His daughter is in college. The driver thought it too risky to drop me off at the bottom of the off-ramp hill to the Pentagon. It just meant I had to walk an extra quarter of a mile to get back here on my way to Crystal City. I brought it up because I held a seat forward of the other slug, making it difficult for him to get out.

As we were going home, a driver took three of us and dropped us off on the other side of McDonald's. We slugs need to standardize where the drop-off point is when we say, "Tackett's Mill!"

Wednesday, 28 October 1991

I was at Tackett's Mill early, right at 0530, the slug start time. Some wait for pickups to start. There was an attractive blonde ahead of me with leather brief and long stylish coat. A big Oldsmobile came out of McDonald's with their lights off, went way down the street to turn around, and came back, still with their lights off. I told the woman and guy in front of her that whoever sits next to the driver makes sure he stays awake. Music was primarily from speaker behind me, left rear. It played Baker and Bird disc jockeys radio station, and no one spoke the entire trip. Each driver makes up their own radio and heater / air conditioning rules. Either they choose it themselves or will sometimes ask the riders what they prefer. Traffic was congested due to an earlier accident already cleared.

Thursday, 29 October 1991

The guy in the Oldsmobile with the headlights off picked us up again. What are the odds? Because we all keep somewhat similar schedules, we tend to ride with a certain set of drivers that pick up that time of morning. Driver took only two short haircut—Marine? Never talked or looked. Drove left lane to Hechinger's then cut in. Despicable not to stay in the longer line for your (our) turn. Drove bumper close, hitting the brakes hard several times, making us strain forward in our seat belts. I don't think this guy is alert in the morning.

When going home, a young black woman with soul music in a big car (Buick Regal?) picked us up. Tried to shift music to other speaker and change to popular music for her riders. She also checked with us to see if we were comfortable or too cold or hot. Dropped us off right behind the "silver bullet" (a parking lot marker) at Tackett's Mill.

Friday, 30 October 1991

Three car accident on I-95. New Jeep-like vehicle driver took Route 1 to Telegraph to Braddock to I-95, which brought us out above the accident area. Worked well, only ten minutes late. About thirty-two degrees, twenty-two with wind chill.

Monday, 9 November 1991

Items left in slug cars are being advertised by signs at the slug line. More often than not, you get the same driver, and they still have your umbrella, briefcase, or gloves.

Pickup order disturbed by first call for Crystal City at which I lunged, but another guy was ahead of me. Then a car for 14th Street? And then the district pulling people out of line in an unruly manner.

Going home. There was a smoker in line; smoke finds non-smokers. I gave the smoker an evil eye stare. Turned down a smoker car ride. Smoker sat in front going home, and he smelled of smoke all the way.

Tuesday, 10 November 1991

Clear, cold. I left home with the garbage truck conspicuously blocking the cul-de-sac throat. They clog the middle of the street to pull garbage cans from all sides. Then about sixth in slug line. Watched my breath rise up while facing full bright moon over McDonald's at Tackett's Mill. Comfortable car, make unknown. Driver in civilian clothes, no coat. Woman slug in front and two of us in back. WMAL news all the way in. Told him I wanted off at the bottom of the exit ramp hill, to no comment.

Going home in a large car, a Buick Regal. The car was ancient with dust all over the gauges, and the driver moved very slow.

Wednesday, 11 November 1991

Light traffic on I-95 as government has off. I drove myself in, all cars going faster than me. All the parking spots open at work; it's spooky that you can park anywhere.

Thursday, 12 November 1991

Waited and was first in line. A car pulled up and asked for Master Chief behind two of us slugs. But then asked for Crystal City, two slugs behind a Navy captain and his wife in a Plymouth Voyager, blue with paneling. We all laughed about being off in the middle of the week, like they did something wrong. Master Chief was going to Orlando and had a Southern dialect. The captain went to the DARPA building on Army-Navy Drive

Going home there was a very long wait, over thirty minutes. There was light rain while waiting in line, but we all had umbrellas. A suit was comfortable with the temperature. The driver took country route through Lorton.

Friday, 13 November 1991

Arrived ten minutes late (about 0540) and what a difference! Lot was half full although I found my usual spot across from the McDonald's drive-through window. Guy in dark truck next to me as usual. Stood in long line, but three cars at a time pulled up. Before they did, I turned to put my back to the wind, contrary to slug convention of facing the street. Gusts to 25 mph with temps in forties. With headlights on slug line, it cast long shadows up the hill (of much fought over Food Lion land). It looked like marching spirits, all thin, dark, and haggard. Silence was again replete in the line. I turned, and the wind shifted momentarily, sending a formation of dancing leaves down the vacant street. Slugs weren't trying hard to get three per car. I passed up one to be able to get out easily at the bottom of the off-ramp on arrival at the Pentagon. Civilian driver in a muffler took three of us. Quiet drive except for heater fan dying halfway up. Sounded like a broken film projector. He fussed with it on and off and varying speed, but it had a problem. As I announced the need to drop off at the bottom of the hill, another slug and driver were going to Crystal City (Crystal Gateway Four, or CG-4) directly across the street from my building! He professed giving up asking for

Crystal City riders. We dropped off the nuisance guy, and I got out at the red light under the Route 1 overpass. Traffic report, as usual, said bumper to bumper from Occoquan to Springfield.

Monday, 16 November 1991

Cold, cold, cold. Marine Captain picked up three. Drove aggressively down left lane to near Hechinger's (hardware store) turn, cutting off a van and getting brights to which he held up his hand. He went around traffic to shoot back in prior to the on-ramp. Baker and Byrd on the radio, then it was switched to some indiscriminate trumpet music. When I gave the bottom of the hill blurb, he said he was going to Crystal City too. Short dropped people (other two) at main intersection, then took a long way around to CG-4 parking meter, and I walked the remainder. Same time as if I had walked.

Tuesday, 17 November 1991

Susan (my wife) drove me to the slug line. The van was in for speedometer repair. About four cars pulled up at once when I was fourth from the end of the line. I asked Oriental driver, "Three?" and he said yes. But as I reached the door handle, someone two cars down yelled out, "Crystal City!" I hesitated, then got in. It would be too disruptive to jump cars. There was a car broken down in one lane, so traffic was backed up. Car was cold when we got in. We listened to Jack Eden at first: "Lay out newspaper on your kitchen table, then tie up your bulbs with plenty of dirt, and put the bulbs on the paper. When they dry, the leaves will fall out. Then make a powder mixture of zinc and sulfur. Clean dirt off the bulbs and massage powder over them." The driver abruptly changed channels and lowered the volume to the point you could just tell it was on. He drove 55 mph, the limit, and turned the heat up. I was roasting in my suit coat and overcoat, but slugs don't complain. The car behind us at the bottom of the hill was doing the same debarking.

Thursday, 19 November 1991

Plymouth Voyager with Captain and his wife pulled up and called for Crystal City. Garfield was hanging from the rearview mirror. Light rain, intermittent. On WTOP news, Jack Eden stated "Fertilize your lawn this weekend." Some people accept this with a shovel of salt.

Getting colder, going home, still in a light drizzle. Short, stocky woman in line ahead of me was complaining to a more business-like woman. We rode home together yesterday in a yellow station wagon. We all got into the same car going home. We were quiet until an accident on Davis Ford, where it becomes Old Bridge, almost making me miss my dental appointment for a failed front tooth crown. The driver made no attempt to try an alternate route.

Friday, 20 November 1991

There was a long wait after I had become head of the line. Cool but no topcoat. I felt I jinxed the line after not pushing for three on the last car. It had only two doors and would be difficult to get out easily at the Pentagon. Other two slugs were hesitant as I let them go first. One slug knew the driver and his people. All three were not in suits and had the demeanor of farmers, hunters, or blue-collar workers. They began with slug's "trip" hunting deer and turkey, but got none. Driver's kids were doing well. WTEL team sports radio all goofy sports talk, football, hockey. Dino Cicerelli (Detroit Red Wings) was playing, Caps (Capitol's hockey) baseball Dennis Eckersley MVP and Cy Young winner.

Monday, 23 November 1991

The captain and his wife asked for Crystal City just after getting in line. This seems inappropriate, but drivers deep select anyone in line if it's more convenient for them at the other end of the commute.

Storm last night was discussed for two minutes until I thanked them, getting out at the "paperclip" building (the window arrangement looked like a huge paperclip standing on end). It was an Army-Navy joint-use building close to the northern end of Crystal City. WMAL on radio, Jack Eden says, "Read poinsettia's instructions carefully. They don't mention liquid fertilizer vice watering to make them last."

Tuesday, 1 December 1991

Drizzle, cold. Long, long, abnormally long slug line. I was fifteenth or twentieth, arriving at 0525. Father of soccer son (Eric) and I talked. Big car! Olds? Elderly woman said not to use left door; latch didn't work. Soccer dad asked, "No way out?" She explained that her son, college age, had taken cap off. Digressed to her twins in a local college. Son at James Mason. Popular music, surprisingly. Dropped off at light on right turn; slow to stop and got out with the car rolling.

Going home. Gray-bearded driver reeked of ketones more than body odor. He asked me to move the paper I was reading so he could see the right rearview mirror.

Wednesday, 2 December 1991

Frost covered the grass. The breath of all the slugs and the exhaust from cars rose in plumes of declared heat sources. The slug line stood in rigid line-up perfection. And stood. And stood. The line again was very long, probably sixty people before I got in a car. We observed a near hit of a slug by a passing car and a pickup almost backed into a van in backing into a parking spot by McDonald's. I got into a large two-door car alone. The driver sounded and acted like Buck Rogers on TV. An older woman was on his right and had to get out to let me in. The car, for a big car, was claustrophobic; my head touched the ceiling, and the front and rear windows were squashed and smaller than normal. The driver wanted to talk, so we did. During the conversation, the woman kept breaking in with

"There it is!" or "That's right again!" The man later said she had lost her glasses in that van, and she stated she had put ads in all the Pentagon bus stops and trash cans with info to contact her but no one had. The driver was a retired Army chief for Apache helicopters. I told him of my retirement and of flying for the Navy over four thousand helo hours flying from ships. He had been in Vietnam and several years in Fort Rucker, about the time I had been at Pensacola as an advanced flight instructor in H-1s. I was extended six months as DoD kept putting off the promised consolidation of the Navy instruction with the Army's at Ft. Rucker. He retired at twenty-six and had started a company with a friend. Said people have no concept of how difficult it is to start a business. We discussed being in DoD procurement and agreed it was an amazing business.

Going home. Very short line. Smoker behind me reeked of it all the way home.

Thursday, 3 December 1991

Yes, I was up late with kinship (2215) (our small church home group). Struggled to get out the door and arrive in the slug line, thirtieth or so, about 0537. But a car pulled up and asked for Crystal City to the consternation of all the slugs in line. Plucked specially from the ignominious fate of an innominate slug. First or second lieutenant in the Marine Corps. He worked at CG-4, but needed to park at the concrete factory. Dropped me and another Crystalite at Crystal Gateway North (CGN)! Right in front of the door! Only problems: (1) he hugged bumpers and made me very anxious coming in and (2) both talked continuously of deployments, amphibs served on, etc. Driver bragged of two six-month deployments on Inchon and Wasp. Second was lousy as crew was not experienced while Marine Detachments knew it all.

Meanwhile, the guy in back with the Tomahawk missile program got a lot of message traffic because they controlled *all* training, launches, and assets. Ford Agency with DPA (contractor) supports the RPV (remotely piloted vehicle) program office. Bragged about how sharp SEALS were and how he turned a unit around that was slack, knocked off early on Friday, etc. for incentives. We were finally saved by our arrival. I don't know how he got his big head out of the car.

Passed three car accident halfway down Davis Ford Road. One car was submarined to another that had only its bumper on the ground. A third car was rear ending the submarined car. All the occupants were standing around. Needless to say, the two lanes to one was causing a backup getting out of Woodbridge. The fire truck stopped us at Occoquan Road, nearly causing an accident to our right as the car even with us stopped abruptly for the truck.

Going home, I was in front of a short, plump, gray-haired woman who is always talkative in the slug line. We got the woman and her child. She kept checking her rearview mirror on me and finally said, "Didn't you coach kids' soccer once?"

I thought, *Uh-oh! I hope this isn't one of the parents I offended!* "Yes," I said reluctantly, and she said her son was Brett Abner. I remembered he was a good player, so I knew I was safe. He had switched to baseball and was happy with it.

Friday, 4 December 1991

A normal, cold morning. Slight southerly breeze that caused the young mulatto Air Force officer to my left to face me, that is perpendicular to the line. It was very disconcerting, having someone face you continuously. He also had a small mustache, like Hitler's. We were well down the line moving slowly when a Navy captain in a troop vehicle called for six! Hitler and I got in last, and I was careful to get the door for getting off first. The guy in the front seat talked with the driver about yesterday's accident, and the two behind us talked about Christmas trees. Us three in the middle were silent. I tuned out the front and tried to listen to the tree story. Seems his father used to get the top of fir trees felled by others and took extra branches. Then at home, he would drill holes for branches to make it fuller. People are always exclaiming what a pretty and full tree we had, and his dad always said we were lucky.

The driver was folksy and very nice. Played classical music with one stop for news. Troops (Marines) were preparing to land, filling out wills, etc.

Friday, going home, I walked to the Pentagon slug line and got in a car right away, but we had to wait for another slug. The walk from CGN to the Pentagon is usually done purposefully but not fast. Today I heard footsteps coming up fast and decided to speed up. He or she might be going to my slug line. I kept this up approaching the I-95 overpass and then decided chances are, like once before, the person is hurrying back to the Pentagon or his car in the lot. I slacked off, and a large-nosed officer surged past. I picked up the pace again, staying just ten yards back. Going through the traffic of the I-95 on ramps, I outsmarted him and took the lead. He virtually ran to get past again, so I let him go. I kept sight of him, though, and stayed ten to twenty yards behind until, yep, he got in my slug line behind one person. I was number three. A white van pulled up, took two, and whisked them home. I waited and waited for the next driver.

Finally, I got the guy who liked to pick up one and get the other rider at the Pentagon for more delay. We waited until a traffic cop moved us, then waited in the parking lot. He stood half out the door, insisting she was always on time, and who hasn't had a boss stop you at the last minute? I had gotten in line at 1530, and now it was close to 1600, and I was still at the Pentagon! I was about to get out and go back to the slug line when his wife got in and drove. The Army officer acted Goosey Loosey. When I initially got in, he said, "Did you hear we're going into Somalia?" I told him the amphibs and Marines were already there. When his wife got in, she said she was delayed for troop movements. Goosey Loosey said, "Who, when, where?" She said she didn't know. I repeated the "news" that the Marines were already there, and he said he hadn't read the paper yet. His wife dropped me off opposite where most drivers drop us, near our cars.

Thursday, 10 December 1991

Winter storm warning! As forecast and well known for a week, the storm hit as I dressed for work. I skipped breakfast to get into the slug line early. I did. It was about 0520, and I was third in line. I fumbled with gloves, a fold-out umbrella, my lunch, and a plastic grocery bag covering my work folders and notebook. The sleet made a neat noise on the umbrella. Almost as soon as I stabilized in line, a large truck-like Jeep pulled up for three. The driver was a smallish woman with an accent of unknown nationality. She drove conservatively and was polite and sociable.

Going home, Guy (that was his name) and his wife (our neighbors) in a Jeep-like vehicle took me and one other slug. The line was only one or two people long. Accident reported on I-95 caused him to take so many side roads I lost track, although we came out on the Springfield bypass road. Then he took a different road to get to Occoquan, via Lorton. Got home in about an hour in heavy wind and rain.

Friday, 11 December 1991

Rushed to get to the slug line, skipping breakfast again and got in a line of cars at the Safeway turn. I knew I had an edge as I had only to snatch my Bible and lunch, leaving the door unlocked. Still, there was a lot of people scurrying to the line. As I approached, two cars were picking up, and the first was waiting for Crystal City. I didn't even have to get in line! Good thing, too, with the rain and blowing wind. Rain had stopped briefly and started again en route. High wind was out of the northeast, and rain/snow continued all day. Just walking between the Crystal City buildings was miserable. (They formed a wind tunnel that increased and directed the wind down the street.)

Monday, 14 December 1991

Cool, but dry. Arrived in line at 0530. About tenth in line. Eric's dad (from kids' soccer) and I talked in line. He drove last Thursday and got a ride Friday. He thought I was hardy for going to the line. A van pulled up and took four. A car for two. Still about fourth or fifth. A minivan pulled up and deep selected for Crystal City. It was the captain and his wife. She was driving, of course. I dozed, eyes closed, and prayed for various areas of my family and listened to Jack Eden describe his friend getting a Fraser fir. It seems it wasn't absorbing the tree preservative. Well, Jack explained, he didn't do the branch test, where you break a branch and see if it's white, still living. If he had, he would have found it white, probably from all the rain the previous week. Thanks, Jack! What a swell tip! The news was of Somalia and whether the gangs should be forced to disarm, although some were doing it voluntarily, probably, I would guess, from watching what happened to Iraq (after we defeated them) and Clinton's economic summit. And how great it was that small shop owners and large corporate executives (like the president of "M" TV) would attend. Obviously, Clinton didn't take a systems management course. It would have taught him only two or three outcomes from meetings: (1) hardened positions, (2) polarized groups, (3) change wasn't likely. We arrived, and the captain said, as he always does, "Have a good day!" To which I replied, but then I can't decide if he meant it for me or directed it toward his wife.

Going home, the slug line dissolved. Cold, gray, and overcast. I was first in line on arrival. Waited ten minutes and the next car had a man and a woman in the front of a four-door sedan. I and a plump Army-enlisted guy got in behind me. I slid next to the hanging uniforms, and he said that it's okay; they need to go to the laundry anyway. So I sat next to his smelly shirts blocking my view all the way home. There was really no place to put them. Traffic stopped halfway down the HOV while regular traffic zoomed by at speed.

Tuesday, 15 December 1991

I arrived at the slug line at 0530. But unlike yesterday, the slugs were out in force. I was about thirty to forty down the line. Eric lined up next to me, and we talked of getting a Crystal City car. Then a van pulled up. It was the captain and his wife! Two Crystal City people, a man and a woman, were ahead of me, but I asked, "Three?" And they said, "Yes." I sat in the back seat by myself. The woman ahead and to the left, a master chief in the Navy in front of me. The master chief knew the captain and immediately launched into a litany of how his law school was going. "I got a B on the test last night. Some left, but I stayed to get my grade." And how "Daddy wasn't paying for it!" Then it was how contractors had parties relative to how his office did it. Said he and his commander were the only military in the office. They lamented coordinating potluck for the Christmas party so the master chief said, "Buy a foot-long sub, sodas, get music, and be done with it!" The captain said, "Yes, that's a lot less hassle." Which was the most I had ever heard him say in many rides. The master chief said he was invited to contractor parties with champagne and really did it up. But he liked what some companies were doing. Taking the $5 gratuity money and donate it to charity. (Who are these guys?) I drifted off in my own thoughts and prayers. When I came back to reality, the master chief was still talking, this time about mast and punishment. Finally, he stopped, and I could just barely hear Jack Eden on the radio. The wife coughed, and the master chief cracked some sort of joke, like you should use that to stay home! And the wife said it was bronchitis. Give me a break. I heard it, and it was nothing. She said she got it from her students. They get better, and then she gives it back to them. Jack Eden said a staffer from WTOP radio was putting a Christmas tree with dirt ball in his house to be planted outside later. He said, "Let me go through this scenario so you will know what to do. Dirt ball in a big tub, but don't bring it in the house. The most you could do would be six days, and it wouldn't be worth it. So leave it outside." Wowzers! He didn't answer the question of how you use it in the house. We arrived, the other two stayed, and I got out before or didn't hear the captain say, "Have a good day!"

Going home. I was getting late in the slug line, ended up about twentieth and 1600. Line moved slow, and it was gray and cold. A large car finally picked up me and the woman behind me. I thought at first it was a black couple, but it turned out an Oriental-looking woman was the driver for the young black guy in the right seat. Uncharacteristic of slugs, the two talked about how they found out about slugging and when they moved to Woodbridge. Both moved about four months ago and still were not familiar with the area. The driver and shotgun were from Ft. Myers, in DC, and, if not for the Pentagon to Ft. Myers problem, could slug too. His car, evidently an expensive BMW, was in the shop. He and she were Army transfer and relocation officials. She, the Oriental woman, spent six years in Germany with her husband. She was directed to the slug line one day, and the slugs told her how the system worked and which line to be in. The older woman to my right was picked up by a taxi at the airport, and the taxi driver picked up slugs to speed the trip south on I-95. I commented the car was very roomy, and the driver said it was a Plymouth Dynasty and she was short, hence the room in back. I-95 northbound was chockablock with what appeared to be a new traffic pattern.

Wednesday, 16 December 1991

Cold and dark, as usual. I got in line about fifteenth at 0530, next to the talking master chief who was holding his hands over his ears. Moments later, like an alerted hunting dog, he suddenly picked up his briefcase. I looked for his signal, and it was the silver Dodge Caravan of the captain and his wife. Sure enough, he pulled up and asked for Crystal City. The master chief and I surged out of line to the other slugs' chagrin. Surprise was, though, that the captain was driving! The master chief asked (the captain not being talkative) and found out the wife was home with a cold. Also surprisingly was that the captain took the Devil's Reach cut-off and drove somewhat aggressively, although he allowed car after car to cut in front of us.

We arrived at 0610, and the captain dropped us off at the Doubletree Hotel to pay for parking.

Coming home. The HOV on lane was changed! Changes in traffic patterns are so rare it was a treat, like opening a present, to drive expectantly. We passed a lot of new construction, including an overpass, but the on-ramp for HOV was the old, old one at Springfield, back in the wrong direction. I sat in front of another guy that arrived ahead of me in line, so I let him chose front or back, and he picked back to sit alone. There was a red strobe light mounted on the dash, and he explained he was an OWL (Occoquan, Woodbridge, Lakeridge) volunteer. I asked what the advantages were for volunteering and if he knew Bob Young, a friend and volunteer also. Yes, he did and another woman firefighter too. The said firefighters were close-knit all over the world. They were given property tax breaks and free county vehicle stickers.

Thursday, 17 December 1991

I'm late! I was determined to get a bowl of cereal down. Left the house at 0529. Rats! I would miss the captain and his wife. They hit the slug line at 0530. The line was thirty-five to forty people long in a light drizzle. As usual, some people don't get wet without an umbrella. At least they don't seem to care if they do. Of course, there is still some confusion in this area for military personnel. A Navy officer below the rank of commander (no egg on his cover), no insignia on his raincoat, got in line next to me, holding a coffee mug but no umbrella. After five minutes of no action, cars began pulling up quickly. As the first car loaded, two more waited. A woman at the head of the line walked forward to load, followed by the talkative master chief who suddenly got in the second car while the woman got in the third, thinking the second was already loaded. The third car had indicated three, so I shouted to the head of the line, "Two more," and they peeled off, the second delaying the third car's departure.

The captain and his wife pulled up and called for Crystal City! I was then about twentieth, so I leaped forward. The wife was back with the captain explaining she had been sick. She reinforced it by saying, yes, she had bronchitis and had gone to Primus. The Primus doctor was Norwegian and commented there was a requirement for the Primus doctors to be foreigners. We briefly discussed Devil's Reach versus the line of cars, but the captain couldn't sell his wife on the quicker route. I mentioned my previous car pool that felt the KFC cut off illegal. We all agreed the really nasty people were the left-lane darters. The captain turned and looked at me for several moments while I spoke, as though he thought, *I might as well look at this guy. We keep getting him!* We discussed parking arrangements, me trying to get my parking pass rented out. But the wife parked at the school on King St., and the captain paid $5 a day under the Doubletree Hotel when she was out. Convenient for him as it was at the northern Pentagon end of Crystal City.

Monday, 21 December 1991

Holiday anomalies! Arrived at 0530 to see the captain and his wife pulling away. I was eight in line. Cold, cold, cold! Clear, stars out. Guy next to me saw a meteor. One car came in fifteen minutes. The slug line stretched the length of the block interminably. I joked with the meteor guy to my right that it appeared slugs don't get a vacation but the drivers did. I put my gloves on. I had my knit cap and umbrella in my trench coat pocket. The bus slowed approaching our line but continued on when the driver saw the slug line was not his bus line. Finally, a Volvo took three of us. The instrument panel was iridescent yellow with orange displays. We fumbled for our seat belts, and I squashed the meteor guy's lunch, which was small to begin with. "Sorry," I said. He moved it. Guy in front seat let it slip, and it made a loud noise against the car, drawing a concerned look from the driver. As we waited at our first light, the radio announced all traffic was good except I-95 northbound, where there was a mechanical emergency in the far-right lane at Lorton. The cars all opted for Route 123 northbound to avoid it. The on-ramp was unusually heavy and slow. We stayed far right and zipped along. It got heavy, and the driver slid left as all traffic stopped. Passed the red emergency lights, a pickup with police, and an ambulance. Off the road. Strange. But traffic was great past the rubberneckers, and I dozed off. Dropped at the bottom of the hill, although the driver was going to Crystal City. As I got out, I suddenly thought as he drove away, "My gloves!" but they had fallen from my lap into the street gutter.

Post-Christmas, New Year's holidays no commuting

At this point, it might be a good time to point out a technique that developed in going home from work because it involved some walking, whereas in the morning we drove to the park 'n' ride lot. One slug did this, and it spread like wildfire. We all started carrying destination signs so that the drivers could pick us up en route to the slug line! I made one up for Tackett's Mill and held it up as I walked to the Crystal City pickup point. This expedited getting home for both the driver and slug. If there weren't enough slugs, one could always finish the drive to the designated line and pick up more. We even got to where we held our signs up in line so you could be "deep selected" for a ride.

Monday, 4 January 1993

Arrived 0530, about fifth in line. Moved three at a time as drivers tried to help with the long line. Clear and cold, forty degrees or so. Jeep Rover picked up guy in back from Minnesota. Only wanted to talk about why they lost to the Redskins in playoffs. Driver abstained. Went to silence halfway there. Driver was going to south Crystal City but had to go to Pentagon first, so I took the turn departure.

Tuesday, 5 January 1993

It had rained heavily early in the morning, but as I drove to Tackett's Mill there, was none. Just a refreshing after spring rain feeling. I was about twelfth in line at 0530 after two guys insisted on backing into a parking spot. After that snafu, we all waited patiently for a ride. Fortunate, I thought that the rain had stopped. Then as we waited, it began to drizzle lightly. It steadily increased in intensity as we all dug for our umbrellas. The guy to my right had his in his briefcase and fumbled frantically as the rain poured down. The cars finally started coming. A Pontiac Grand Am. Comfortable. I was third to get in, rear left. The driver moved his seat up to accommodate me. I dozed and listened to the radio. No words were ever spoken among the four of us. Michael Dodd, a child killer in Washington State, was hanged, and a reporter described in minute and excruciating detail the hanging. I was released at the red light after a right turn at the bottom of the hill to the Pentagon. Pouring rain. Rivers of water ran everywhere. I cut under the Double Tree Hotel as a flight crew loaded in a van. Then back into the rain, arriving at work wet everywhere but upper torso.

Going home. Arrived at 1540, and there were three cars queued up! Got in a station wagon with two guys. The driver said he usually slugged, but it seemed every time he picked up slugs, there were none. Driver kidded with shotgun guy all the way to Tackett's Mill. The rear speakers were loud, and along with the car highway noise, I could only pick up some of the joking. Besides, I was reading the paper about NASA's thirty-million-dollar toilet and former DC mayor Marion Barry's car being stolen. Traffic was heavy and slow, and the driver bailed out of the HOV early. The normal traffic lanes were sometimes faster than HOV as many illegal single drivers jumped on it. He must have been single because he joked with us about being in a car pool with only women as he dogged a car that had five girls in it. That car changed lanes to the right inside lane, and he changed lanes to the far right. I observed him ogling as I looked up from the newspaper. I glanced over at the other car to see what reaction he was getting. In the right rear, a woman moved her head also to see. It was someone that had worked in an office next to the one I worked in two years ago. She waved, and I waved back. The crew, driver, and shotgun were consternated. I didn't remember her name, only seeing her at work.

Wednesday, 6 January 1993

Winter again. Cloudy, cold, and dark. About twentieth. As there was an early rush to the line, it was slow starting. It moved two at a time until I got to the head of the line. Numerous vans and empty cars passed us. They joked it was because of them. The line grew to the corner, about sixty people in formation. The interesting thing about the slugs, though, was that we didn't stand in a line like we were buying tickets, but all faced the street so that we were in line shoulder to shoulder. To see the pickup cars coming, I guess. A black woman stood to my right and laughed as we joked about getting a Burger King sandwich passed to us as the end of the slug line was getting close to it. Finally, the lead two were picked up. The woman and I got in a Land Rover. It was the guy that worked at the south end of Crystal City. He didn't recognize me, though, and asked where I wanted to be dropped. I asked for Crystal Gateway North, close enough.

Going home. Rear seat of a small, small Honda Civic. Read paper and could tell the driver and woman to his right talked, but car and highway noise prevented me from hearing.

Thursday, 7 January 1993

Dark, dry, and cool. Lined up about twelfth, next to same black woman as yesterday. The slug process ran in periods where you had the same timing as the drivers or other slugs. In fact, today the line looked just like yesterday's with the same people. Again, it quickly increased to forty or fifty slugs before pickups began. Drivers were stingy, picking up only what they needed, no more. A car pulled up behind a loading van, and the driver made a gesture. Usually, the drivers hold up the number of fingers for passengers desired or roll the window down and shout the destination: "Pentagon" or "Crystal City" or "State Department." A lot of people worked clear across town at the State Department. This guy made no gesture and left the window up. Finally, the van moved, and he looked to the head of the line, annoyed (I was fifth now) that no one was loading. He gestured two, and as they hurriedly got in, I gestured three. No response. The next car loaded, then the black woman motioned one more in the back. The driver had MIX 107.3 FM on the radio. Stacey Binn, we learned, was welcomed back, and Jack Diamond asked what exciting thing happened on vacation. She replied not in my life. Iraq was being defiant against UN sanctions to remove anti-aircraft missiles along the specified parallel. No word was spoken the entire trip, except the driver asked the slug to his right if he didn't pick him up yesterday. The slug replied, "Yes." I asked for drop-off at the bottom of the hill at the Pentagon turn, and he felt it too dangerous, so he dropped me at the off-ramp side of the intersection.

Going home was a disaster! NAVAIR (Naval Air Systems Command) has a saying which is frequently invoked. It was appropriate today as our customer asked at 1400 for a brief to be done by 0900 tomorrow when he knew he had this requirement yesterday. The saying is "Poor planning on your part does not constitute an emergency on my part!" But it does in the contractor support business. I worked until 1745, at which time I decided the 1845 VRE train would not get me close to Tackett's Mill. I literally ran to the slug line. It was dark out, and the slug line at 1800 was twenty people long. And there were single driver cars queued up for HOV to end. That is they were waiting *with slugs in sight* for the HOV period to end so they could jump on HOV legally by themselves. That's how bad drivers want to drive alone and not be bothered with picking up and dropping off riders. This was not especially helpful. We die-hard slugs wanted a Good Samaritan, or several, to save us. Until it was obvious the bus was needed. Here I was unprepared for what happened next. Okay, I thought, I didn't get a free ride, but I would pay and have a comfortable bus seat home. By the time the bus pulled up, the slug line had joined the bus line for Woodbridge. But the bus only had seven or eight seats. The collector got out, and I asked if it was $5. He said it was unless someone sold be tokens for $3. No one offered, thinking, *I'm sure, that this guy deserves this.* I got on the bus and stood all the way to the first Woodbridge stop. It was an interminable wait. Traffic was heavy (it gets worse exponentially), with a couple of accidents. Plus it was after six, and HOV was lifted. Standing I could see only a few feet in front of the bus and cars to the side. Seated people slept, read, or chatted. Two women to my left spoke continuously for the hour it took to reach Woodbridge even though it was bus policy to limit talking so that riders could sleep. I was surprised at how smooth riding the bus was. The collector interrupted twice. My car was one of three left in the McDonald lot at Tackett's Mill. It was 1910.

Friday, 8 January 1993

Continuous, steady, cold rain. Pickups were slow, although I was eighth in line. I had the opportunity to study the rain striking the pavement as we slugs stood at umbrella attention. Some drops hit harder and explode more or perhaps are larger than others which coalesce into the surface water without much of a ripple. I was one person to the left of Kevin (soccer Dad) and right of a shorter, stocky black woman. She and I joked about the drivers taking the day off. A van took the woman to my right and me. It wasn't a Plymouth as the seat belts weren't on the right. As I felt to the left, I pulled a belt, and it was my trench coat. I felt right to left again. Again, my belt. Finally, with some streetlight, I saw the woman had taken mine. I said, "Excuse me, you've got my belt!" Without a word, she released the belt and grabbed hers. The driver and shotgun position were dark jacketed military personnel. The driver had high cheekbones and female close-cropped hair. In the rearview mirror, she looked like a guy. He or she was very tense driving, sitting on edge and gear shifting. The windshield wipers were on intermittent as we drove super cautiously. I thought at first it was a Good Samaritan, but he or she carried politeness to new extremes and our detriment. She or he left a large space in front of her van for every swinging car to cut in. The last straw was the pickup at the on ramp. Incredible. If he or she let anymore in front of us, we would be back at our houses. She or he played WMZQ on the radio, and it was crystal—CD—clear. The music wailed in country music simplicity, "Don't walk out the door, or I'll be on the floor!" or "I've got holes in my life, holes in my clothes, holes in my teeth, if taken together a bottomless pit!"

She or he dropped me at the light in a right-hand turn. When she or he spoke, surprisingly she was feminine. I contemplated this as I walked in the rain to Crystal Gateway North and the start of the Crystal City Underground (tunnel to shops and food court).

Monday, 11 January 1993

Fifteenth or so. Snow still on the grass with freezing rain forecast. Light slick ground coating in places. Cars arrived quickly when they did come. I and two other slugs got into a nice, comfortable car. I was on back seat, right side. The driver asked us to buckle up, which slugs do routinely as our only defense for whoever is driving. Listened to WQXY (Mix) 106.1 and their berating of the Redskins. Disc jockey went to game, and he critiqued it. News. Unnamed Iraqis stole back their weapons from Kuwait. Is anybody watching them? I complimented the driver on his car; it was a Camry and very nice.

Tuesday, 12 January 1993

In line at 0525! Light traffic to Tackett's Mill. Parked in front of the drive-through window, for security, although I'm convinced the window teller would likely watch a theft take place and not get involved. Pickups came rapidly, three at a time. An Air Force (blue fore and aft cap and leather flight jacket with SAC emblem) was behind me. It's curious the Navy didn't allow us pilots to wear our leather flight jackets off base because it was considered flight gear. As we stood in the cold, misty, very foggy weather I checked, and you could easily see your breath. SAC's breath could be seen to drift over me no matter how I shifted my position. Didn't smell or anything, but I just didn't like the idea. We got a Volvo with an Army colonel driver and Navy captain in shotgun. I recognized the combo as I had ridden with them before. SAC breath and I went for the near door, stopped, went for it and stopped again. He said he didn't care, and I realized I'd better take this door to get off at the bottom of the hill near the Pentagon. I didn't mention his breath. The radio was on, but I dozed from being up with the baby all night. No words were spoken.

Going home in the slug line at 1540. Surprise! While there was a long line for Potomac Mills, there was only one woman for Tackett's Mill. As I approached, a woman pulled up in a Jeep of some sort. I never did get the make of the car. It was thin walled, however, and easily transmitted road noise. The slug woman was in a long coat and blondish, neck length hair, got in the shotgun seat. I got behind her in the right rear. The driver was a brunette with glasses who drove in her stocking feet. And drive she did! Like a bat out of hell! She had to be late for an appointment as we weaved through and past most traffic. We arrived at Tackett's Mill at 1605, and when I walked into our house at 1615, the kids' comment was, "How come you're home so early?"

Wednesday, 13 January 1993

I left the house at 0510 to drive to National Airport; the flight left at 0650, but I still had traffic to beat. It was fast and free-flowing in HOV until two miles south of the Belvoir exit at the gas tank farm. I was in the second lane from the right. The '81 Toyota Starlet strained doing 60 or 65 mph, so I liked to do 55 mph, which most of the I-95 traffic wouldn't tolerate and pass me. Other likeminded cars were ahead, including a pickup truck. All of a sudden, the pickup hit his brakes! I did, too, and because I had maintained a safe distance, I snaked back and cross in the lane as I hit the brakes hard. This time, two cars collided even with the pickup, which slowed to about thirty and kept going. I followed but swung left some as I observed six or so cars collided together. Glass and metal were on the road. Apparently, a car had stopped in the far right lane or had a fender bender.

Tuesday, 19 January 1993

A day sandwiched between Martin Luther King Jr.'s celebrated birthday (not actual, but government Monday) and the inauguration of Bill Clinton as president. Arrived in the slug line in good shape, at 0530. I was the second car to park in the row closest to McDonald's. That was a tip off as there is always a compliment of cars already there. I was eighth in line. Partly cloudy. Cold, very cold. After ten minutes, an Oldsmobile pulled up, asking for Crystal City! I leaped forward, grabbing for the front door. She unlocked it as I pulled. Still locked. She tried again, as did I. Still locked. Finally, I left my hand off while she sorted it out. A guy got in the back. The woman spoke with a British accent and was gray-haired, appearing to be family should be fairly old. She spoke lively, however, and she and I conversed all the way in.

Her car pool was depleted from people taking the "middle" day off. I told her my opinion—that I wish I had a government job so I could get so much paid time off. I said I felt the Compressed Work Schedule (CWS) policy was not working as intended, with employees using the CWS day to do home errands to not interfere with work on other days. The concept was four days a week you would work extra hours and then not have to come in Friday, saving one commute. Instead, they were using the day to extend their weekend *and* still taking off during the week to run errands. She assured me she used it as intended. The other requirement was that someone from the office could cover your work for you while you were out on CWS. But most offices did not have backups, and you could not contact that person on that day or expect to get work done. Someone in the office would answer the phone and say, "Sorry, he or she is out today, and they are the only one who can respond so please call back Monday." She was a secretary for NAVSUP, Navy Supply, so it didn't matter much. She was from Britain, sixty-one years old, and her husband retired at sixty-six, from the Post Office Headquarters on L'Enfant Plaza.

She said her husband liked the cold, and she froze in the car with him. She apologized for the heat coming on late. She lived only down the road, and the car didn't have time to warm up. She was early enough she didn't need to pick up slugs but remembered when they didn't have a car in Canada and she waited, freezing in the cold. Her husband kept fifty-eight at home. I didn't know if that meant he had a lot of relatives or managed an apt complex. I asked, and she said, "No, fifty-eight degrees on the thermostat." He turned it up to seventy degrees when she got home. Since she worked at NAVSUP, I asked if she knew a former car pooler Kevin Fitzpatrick, and she did. I briefed her on what our car pool rides were like. On arriving at work few people were in and many left early, not a good deal for slugs, who were confined to the slug pickup times.

Wednesday, 20 January 1993

Inauguration Day for Bill Clinton. Government personnel were encouraged to stay home to decrease the flood of people attending the ceremony at the Capitol Building. I stayed home as there would be no one to work with.

Thursday, 21 January 1993

Very cold! Out the door at 0525. In line by 0535. Parking was a puzzle at first as all the end spots next to McDonald's were taken, including my usual spot in front of the drive-through window. As I stood eleventh in line, shivering, I could see in the parking lot lights. The first row was coned and ribboned off limits. For what, it wasn't clear. A car pulled up, and it looked like a gray-haired Dorothy (from *The Wizard of Oz*). She asked for Crystal City! The number one guy in line, and I got in. Dorothy still (I had ridden with her before) had a bad raspy cough. The number one guy fumbled to get the window up as we waited for the light to change. He couldn't find the electric window button. Finally, Dorothy said, "Oh, just say *window*!" She apologized for not being awake. Great! This is the person that's going to get me safely to work. She took the Occoquan cutoff (to get farther up I-95 before joining) but not the Devil's Reach turn. Instead she went to the road past the defunct Ames Shopping Center, normally a busy area. I don't know what prompted the move, but it worked. The Route 1 on-ramp to I-95 was down to one lane for construction. She sat at the first light after green for some time. I was going to comment when the car behind honked. That and other waits for cars that were turning indicated she still wasn't alert.

Ride home was in right rear of a new car driven by a divorced mother of three whom I had met at soccer and had worked in Naval Air Systems Command (NAVAIR). We talked while the black Air Force officer to my left opened his briefcase to get out reading material. We talked about soccer versus baseball versus football for our kids, while she interrupted with a car phone call to home and remind someone to bag the newspapers. We discussed that, too, my kids having run a Potomac News route last summer. We talked about her car phone some and then entered into slug silence as we drove through a steady, cold drizzle.

Friday, 22 January 1993

Some of the parking lot barricades at Tackett's Mill were down and parking almost normal. It was cold, misty, and foggy. I was about twelfth to fifteenth in line, and no cars were picking up. It was 0535. I had noticed a guy and girl getting out of a jeep-like vehicle, she kissing a guy who got in to drive away. The other guy and girl got in line next to me, on my left (we were in slug line formation, facing the street and loading right to left). They were obviously new to the slug procedures and slug line protocol. They didn't stand at strict attention, facing the street with stoic resolve. Instead, the woman with dark hair faced the guy and moved around, talking incessantly. He spoke occasionally. He had blond hair and glasses. Both seemed about late twenties. Their acting lively and energetic was not apropos to line decorum. Then Dorothy pulled up, and I leaped out. From the beginning of the line, the same guy as yesterday got in shotgun. (As noted earlier, we, the slugs and drivers, had periods when we all had the same timing.) Dorothy apologized for the car being cold again, but at least the window was up. She coughed occasionally all the way in as I dozed. She sounded a little bit better. I arrived at work by 0610.

Monday, 25 January 1993

Partly cloudy, windy. Perfectly on schedule, up at 0450, cats fed, breakfast of cereal and bananas and orange juice. Out the door at 0520. In slug line at 0530, eighth in line. One car making a pickup as I arrived. The slug line mood was professional, somber, serious, and silent. Uncomfortably cold, about forty degrees, with wind chill to thirty. I said Hi to the guy I lined up with as we had seen each other repeatedly. Above the McDonald's and Tackett's Mill lights, I could make out a couple of stars. A car in the drive-through had headlights in the McDonald's line. Then Dorothy pulled up in her old Oldsmobile. Asked for Crystal City, and I was the only one to leap in. This always led to an awkward moment as now we had to ask for Pentagon riders, probably in the front of the line. To blunt that feeling we asked for two, although I later learned Dorothy was perfectly willing to forego the Pentagon as we could still make the HOV before or near the 0600 start time. All you had to do was be on it by 0600, and you could travel the length of HOV without fear of getting a ticket. The head of the slug line got in. A Navy chief to my left, an Air Force colonel in front in shotgun. Neither spoke until saying thanks in a sarcastic manner at the Pentagon drop-off. Dorothy had taken the Occoquan–Horner Road cut expeditiously. While idling at Route 123 and Route 1, the right car body parts made a noise from rusted parts or what I couldn't discern but was now familiar with. After dropping the Pentagon schmucks off, Dorothy became disoriented, and we ended up cutting through the south parking lot to head back to Crystal Gateway 3.

At the Pentagon, I was third in line going home at 1530. As I got in an Air Force colonel's Buick Park Avenue I asked if they caught the CIA shooter yet. I had heard on the radio a madman stood at an intersection and mowed down people as they turned into the CIA parking lot. Descriptions of the man were sketchy as everyone was concerned with where he was pointing the gun, an automatic weapon. Then the news, WTOP, mentioned President Clinton was meeting with the chiefs of staff on gays in the military. We were all (three slugs and the driver) against what Bill was doing. Besides, the driver said, it has to go through Congress to be approved.

Monday, 1 February 1993

Post Super Bowl Sunday. Arrived 0525, ninth in line. I faced the trees, away from the street, as the wind was brisk and cold. The other slugs stood in rigid silence, oblivious to the wind. We moved quickly, and soon I and another slug got in behind a pair of friends who talked all the way to work. An Army colonel was in the right seat, and an Army officer in civilian clothes, civvies, in the left, or driver's seat. The radio provided a popular music backdrop for the conversation: "Took my six-year-old son to Chinn Center, and he had the best time. They have swimming lessons I may get him in. Right now, he just likes to climb on Dad." The colonel responded with, "I know we had great indoor pools in Germany!" (Seems like most Army personnel take at least one overseas assignment in Germany as it is what they all talk about.) Civvy said, "Yeah, Wiesbaden had a Jacuzzi, a wading pool, a knee-deep pool, and two large pools. Chinn reminded me of that." (The Chinn Center—we know because we were there when they built and named it—was named after a former slave who reportedly lived in the area.) The Super Bowl, while discussed extensively on the radio, was ignored. So was politics. Strictly all about my son and soccer. "They have indoor soccer, and I got him enrolled in outdoor soccer." The colonel asked if he had a phone number to find out more as he wanted to enroll his son too. Civvy dropped me at the end of the off-ramp to the Pentagon, very strange. I arrived at work at 0615.

Going home. It was still very wind-chilled cold. As I approached the Pentagon bus stop, I could see there was a long slug line to Potomac Mills. But no one in the Tackett's Mill line. I was glad. It was much too cold to stand outside. One person got in a car, stopped in the parking lot as I approached, and a woman motioned for one more rider. An elderly black man was in back as I climbed in the right front seat. A young woman was driving. We all exchanged comments on the cold and glad to be out of it, then entered slug silence. I read a retired officer and *CompuServe* magazine. Traffic moved well, and I got to my car and home in good shape by 1615. The black man asked the woman driving if he could go further. She declined, so I offered to take him another couple of miles in my direction.

Tuesday, 2 February 1993

Twenty-below wind chill! I arrived at McDonald's at 0530, but no one was at the No Parking sign where we queue up. By the time I reached it, one guy was already shivering there. Soon there were five of us, clearly not the usual slugs. Only the true any-weather slugs. The wind was from the northeast so we could stand facing the proper direction, the street, or west. Finally, a Bronco XLT pulled up and took three of us. He was a military driver with very close-cut hair. No words were spoken except I commented it would be a good day to stay home. To which a slug in the back said, "You can say that again!" I almost did as the driver seemed not to hear. He took the usual Jefferson Davis to Route 123 route but approaching the on-ramp for I-95, he abruptly hauled out to port (left) and went Route 1. Traffic was backed up on I-95 and the on-ramp. It was a good move. We listened to popular music as he sped to the Pentagon. I arrived at work at 0610.

Going home. Clear, windy, still very cold. Arrived sixth in line. It moved quickly, and soon I and a military officer, the last two in line, climbed into a van with captain's seats instead of bench. I didn't determine the make, but it wasn't a Plymouth Voyager or Ford Astro. Roomy, though. I was in back by the sliding door and the Air Force officer, a captain by his blue jacket and rank insignia, like railroad tracks. A big guy was driving, also Air Force, but had gold oak leaves, a major, equivalent to a lieutenant commander in the Navy. It's a curious observation to make that all the services have similar rank structure except the Navy. And captains in the Air Force and Army make good use of the fact anyone who doesn't know them has to assume the higher rank of Navy captain when responding to "a captain." There was a large wooden mug holder velcroed to the dash, and we commented on that briefly. As we listened to the radio the two Air Force officers struck up a conversation while I read writers magazine. Then we noticed the I-95 regular traffic was chockablock. The radio announced the most blessed of HOV events: car on fire in the center of two lanes, blocking regular traffic southbound and freeing HOV traffic through the usual Springfield congestion. As we passed the car fire, it was an old big bomber of a car, the front end charred. Hard to believe the driver stopped in the middle of the road, but fire is scary, and explosion a possibility. Firemen and trucks were on the scene, and a few cars on either side were squeezing by. It developed the driver was retiring in ninety days and had already started a mail order sporting goods store. I couldn't hear much due to road noise and radio, but he already had a mailing list established and was eager to start his business. Said the scary part was opening the store door and waiting for customers to come in. We arrived shortly after 1600 at Tackett's Mill.

Wednesday, 3 February 1993

Twenty-two degrees cold, but not windy, making it seem warmer than yesterday. As I pulled into the McDonald's lot, a Volvo station wagon ahead was doing multiple maneuvers to back in. I whipped around and parked next to the pickup with a guy always sitting there, waiting. I think the Volvo driver was miffed, but "Park the thing already; I want to get in line!" As I stood fifth in line, I noticed all the cars parking closest to McDonald's drive-through were all facing away, toward the parking lot, ostensibly for a quick get-away this afternoon. A recognizable Air Force major lined up to my left, commenting to someone on my right it was much warmer and how yesterday showed who the true slugs were. The third car soon pulled up behind the second, and the major and I got in. Some officer in a sweatshirt with Army logos also got in. I-95 traffic was dealing with a Dumfries vehicle fire and accidents at the Springfield off-ramp and Horner Road. lieutenant colonel, gray hair, was in the right seat that I had ridden in with a few days ago. They talked non-stop while we slugs maintained strict verbal silence. Today's subjects, over the radio's 107.3 FM on the rear speaker, were office spaces, weather, kids, and traffic. The driver had moved into a Ft. Meyer office that had tombstones stacked for Arlington Cemetery! They moved them into the hall to get rid of them. The interior walls were coming down as a study determined modular furniture was more efficient. Weather was improving, they decided. The lieutenant colo-nel, this time, talked about his three kids, all of whom have different personalities. For instance, one daughter gets up at 0500 for school at 0700, to fix her hair, etc. He was appreciative of the difference. They discussed yesterday's traffic blockage from the car fire. I asked for the bottom of the off-ramp hill for drop-off again. For the first time, the driver and passenger looked to see who was "again." Then the driver stated he recalled the voice and drop-off. The lieutenant colonel asked if I was metro bound, and I explained, no, Crystal City. The walk to the office was uneventful except a large van cut in front of me as I walked in the crosswalk, with a pedestrian Walk sign on. I banged the side of the van with my fist as he passed. It stopped shortly, and the guy who got out followed me into Crystal Gateway 3 and the elevator, saying nothing. He had to be aware I had banged his van, and I waited to explode on him. Not a word, and I got off on the third floor without a fight.

Going home. Weather was balmy. Slug line about twenty peo-ple long! Finally, I got in back left seat with two other slugs. The driver was Air Force, as was the slug in the front right, shotgun, position. They talked about duty stations at one point, causing the slug woman to my right to speak up and say "We were there too," obviously referring to her family. I had my Oriole's gym bag of running gear, a large shopping bag with baby clothes a woman at work had given me for our daughter Megan. And I was holding my trench coat. It was all between or on my legs. Slug woman put her leather attaché case in the space between us, causing me to wonder why I suffered the lack of room. I had learned early on that was the recipe for forgetting something in the slug car. It was a Ford Taurus sedan, however, and comfortable to ride in. No traffic accidents or incidents on the way.

Thursday, 4 February 1993

Gosh, we spend our whole life working! I arrived in the slug line at 0528, but already, twenty slugs were there! I noticed the Volvo station wagon was already positioned, his maneuvers completed. Must be waiting for a car pool. Cars pulled up, and the line moved well until I got to the head of the line. Everyone behind you sees you as the obstacle to getting to work, especially if you take a long time getting a ride. Bus riders routinely cross the street and queue up about thirty yards up the street. They usually move past McDonald's and then cross, well clear of the slug troops in rigid street-facing formation. One elderly man, however, seems to have a tick against slugs. He crosses aiming directly at the slug line as though looking for an audience. Walking down the line as though to say, "In your face, take the bus, slugs. I pay to ride to work!" Or like a reviewing officer inspecting his troops. He gets very near the slugs who are heel to the grass on the side opposite the street. It's obvious he's making a statement like "You're disgusting" and "Bus riders have ethics!" Finally, a Chrysler LeBaron pulled up, and an Air Force colonel drove us to work. A big black woman and I in the right rear and an older white woman, left rear. The car was like new, with colorful illuminated little instrument displays. The window visor on my side had a leather holder of some sort. I didn't like having something to come down in my face in an accident, but I am a slug, and I just tolerate it. Traffic moved smoothly, and I arrived at work easily.

Going home. Ten or so of us slugs were in line. Clear and sunny, but not warm enough to take off my trench coat. Three of us got into the XLT Bronco I had ridden to work in twice before. The driver in white long-sleeved shirt with short hair must have been a Navy chief by his blouse (Navy for jacket). I sat in back, on the left after the difficult climb past the front seat, moved forward. A short woman got in to my right and had a tough time with the obstacle course (seat and height). The guy who sat up front talked with the driver as I read John from the Bible, and the woman dozed, head down. The Bronco still had that; I'm sitting high, and the gears are tight, sensation with loose-fitting seat belts. Because of the slug line and my late arrival in it, I didn't get back to McDonald's until 1615.

Friday, 5 February 1993

Mondays and Fridays are usually good commute days as many government employees have one or the other off as part of the compressed work schedule. You work an extra hour a day and then stay home one of those days. A LCDR friend from church, Mark, got in line to my left. I was fifteenth (but who is counting?) at 0533. The line moved slowly, and we talked about what the people entering the service (military) were going to do. My NROTC (Navy Reserve Officer Training Corps) having sent a brochure with a woman XO (executive officer) and a class of over three hundred. Mark gave up waiting for a slug car when the bus came, a sure thing, but not free. Two minutes later, cars pulled up quickly. It wasn't uncomfortably cold in my trench coat. It was supposed to reach the low sixties today. A large Oldsmobile took two of us, and as I got in the shotgun position, I realized it was a mistake, as the guy in the back seat said, "How's OPM?" to the driver (OPM means Office of Personnel Management). They knew each other and talked incessantly all the way in, with something worse than country Western music played in the background. Slugs are used to and hardened for mental abuse of all kinds. Then someone in the car released gas silently, and I began to wonder what was left to assault. They had both been through flight training and the NECEP program, whereby college graduates can take eight or ten weeks of what we get in the NROTC program over four years and three summer deployments. Classes and physical fitness. We in the NROTC and the Naval Academy grads all disliked them for getting what we paid much more dearly for. They reminisced about their drill sergeants by name and who was strict and who was unfair. "One short black guy, Alby, replaced Stokes and must have been Gossett's prototype for the movie *An Officer and a Gentleman*." And Ramos. The driver said he had committed suicide, blew his brains out. At the time, he had chased the women cafeteria workers. The back seat guy said Sanders had been tried for throwing a recruit over the seawall. A civilian in Pensacola was driving by and reported it. Turned out the recruit was suffering from heat stroke, and Sanders helped him the best way possible by rapidly cooling him in the bay. Stokes was brought up on charges of beating some recruit almost to death. Both had been through flight school in '74. I was probably a helicopter flight instructor there, then at Whiting Field. The back-seat guy went through Whiting and then went VQ (jets). The driver went to Corpus Christi, Texas, and VP (prop, or propeller) training. No navigation, though, they stopped the class before his. VQ guy went to survival, escape, rescue, and evasion (SERE) school and seemed eager to talk about it but didn't when the driver said the east coast pipeline didn't allow him to although he had orders at one time. He guessed he didn't need it going down in Iceland. The news in the background was of the family leave bill passing Congress and the gay debate to continue, unattached, as a rider to the leave bill. They discussed the consequences, separate showers for gays, women, etc. Traffic in the HOV lanes slowed almost to a stop for no reason, near Glebe Road, close to Crystal City. Five miles to go. I had acted like I was dozing but sat up as we slowed; it gets your attention. It's funny, but even with your eyes closed, you can tell when someone turns to speak toward you. So I could tell when he looked at me.

Monday, 8 February 1993

Couldn't sleep after about 0400. Work anticipation, I think. I worked in one office where we all came to find out that late on Sunday, just like in school, a feeling of preparation and requirement (dread?) dominated us.

So I got out the door early and was sixth in line at 0525. The cold air allowed us to view our breath as we stood in slug attention, facing the street. After ten or so minutes, a car pulled up and took two. Then three. As the three got in a four-wheel-drive vehicle, the door seat was pulled forward, causing some delay. As they sorted it out, In-Your-Face came by. I had to back up to keep him from stepping on my toes as he circumnavigated the boarding slugs. Then it was over. Like a play from the line of scrimmage, it was confusing and over quickly. First in line, I stared down the headlights of the cars in the McDonald's drive-through.

A Volvo pulled up for three. The car was still cold, so he hadn't come far. I got in shotgun, commented we needed a few more volcanoes to cause warming as I belted myself in. Slugs always use the seat belts as it is our only defense against an unknown driver's skill or lack thereof. The belt buckle was illuminated, a pleasant, unexpected surprise. The car was a stick shift, sort of unusual for a luxury car. The driver, an Army colonel, almost bald, agreed. Not another word was spoken until I asked to be let out at the bottom of the off-ramp. Traffic moved smoothly, and the car warmed up nicely, without the typical sudden blast of hot air going too hot. There was a whirring noise that at first I thought was a heater fan. Then I thought I heard the radio on, but barely audible. Then I sorted it out as a cassette rewinding. When done, the colonel played it; classical music, heavy on the violins. An attempt, I think, to soothe the savage beast. He turned at the bottom of the off-ramp and dropped me off past the stoplight. It was 0600. I could see this was one of those days everything went super well. I got two up elevators when I pressed one button. The elevator, one of eight, was closest to the office. The security light was off, so I was not required to fumble for a key.

Going home. I was the only one in line as the previous car loaded. The Potomac Mills line stretched down the bus island. After several minutes, a small two-door car pulled up, covered with bird droppings. As I climbed in the back, I recognized the driver and almost got out. Now it's an unspoken rule the drivers take care of whatever business they need to before picking up slugs. But this guy—I knew from past experience—picked up his slugs first so that his wife would not have to wait. Just as slugs would. He said, "Just got to pick up my wife, just take a minute." We waited at the bus stop near the Pentagon until she suddenly beat on the trunk. The driver got out, helped her with the trunk, and she assumed the driver's position! She apologized for being late; last time we did this she was late big time, fifteen minutes. I resumed reading the Bible, Job, while they talked occasionally going home. The radio was never turned on.

Tuesday, 9 February 1993

Seventh in line at 0525. Cold! Radio later said twenty-five degrees, with wind chill to thirteen degrees. It felt colder. The Air Force captain to my right shivered violently. He had only his fore and aft cap and a summer-weight, blue jacket on. I had my heaviest wool suit, lined trench coat and gloves, and I was still cold. It wasn't difficult to empathize with him. A civilian lined up to my left, with knit cap and hands in pockets. He wheezed and sniffled and spit in the grass behind us. He was sick! Another slug hazard. As with any mass transit, we have no control over who sits next to you. In-Your-Face came by walking with a friend and steered inside of the slug line. After fifteen minutes, a four-wheel-drive Jeep picked the captain and me up. He got in back. Darn Jeeps! Even belted in I felt I was sitting high and leaning forward. Sort of like I was on a spring-mounted seat just waiting for launch through the windshield. WTOP news radio played the latest: reduction in White House staff without letting anyone go, several gun murders in schools, and Governor Wilder's gun control bogged down in the state assembly. I arrived at work at 0610.

Going home. Man and woman in a four-by-four, waiting. Read John from the Bible while they conversed unintelligibly.

Wednesday, 10 February 1993

Sixth in line at 0530. Still cold. Probably twenty-five degrees again, but little wind, no wind chill. Two of us slugs got in a small, innominate four-door car with two Air Force captains. (Keep in mind the proportions of each of the services in the Pentagon, mostly Air Force.) They talked in low voices, not discernible, while the rear speakers droned, with only an occasional word understandable. We had a couple of abrupt jerky stops. Enough to fear what state the young, short, blond-haired driver with glasses was in.

Thursday, 11 February 1993

There is a DC landfill at Lorton, just across the Occoquan River from Lakeridge so that standing in the slug line at Tackett's Mill we were not far from it. On some days—I'm sure this was one—the easterly winds brought the putrid sweet smell over the area. It was very pronounced as I walked to be eleventh in line at 0525. Ten minutes later, there were over twenty slugs behind me. Stars were still out, and our breath was not as evident. As we waited in rigid formation, heels aligned on the eastern edge of the sidewalk, the talkative Air Force guy to my left commented to someone to my right, "Long line this morning! Well, tomorrow's rain will take care of that!" As though he owned the slug line or he was the only one who could withstand rain. A discussion on Clinton's first Town Hall meeting began to my left with several people. I didn't see it, but it seems despite a carefully screened audience, the first question was on gays in the military and the second on the middle class, and it went downhill from there.

By 0540, a newish car (it turned out to be a Camry) picked me and the civilian next to me. It was the Army guy in civvies (a blue-and-red jacket) with the lieutenant colonel! Still his season with me.

What are the odds? Where did the others go? The captain and his wife, wheezing Margaret and other regulars at the same time? Civvie's first comment, as always, was "Please buckle up."

He and the lieutenant colonel discussed the consequences of the European force reductions from Brigade or Battalion to Division strength. Their conversation intermittently broke through the rear speakers on 107.3, popular music with DJ Diamond in the morning.

There was 40 percent chance of freezing rain expected tonight, 100 percent tomorrow. Bert mentioned those were good odds. The slug to my right slumped and slept. Michael Jackson was interviewed, and it turns out he is not trying to bleach his skin but has a disorder that is making him turn white. He has had only two plastic surgeries to his nose and no other part of his body. And as for dates, he had a crush on Diana Ross and now is dating Brooke Shields. Good PR move, Brooke! I was at my desk at 0615.

Going home, the slugs discussed the approaching ice storm expected tomorrow. Older woman driver with fingers covered with rings. An Air Force officer to my left and a slug in front of me, shotgun. Radio on a popular channel, no talking the entire route.

Friday, 12 February 1993

Outer Loop of the beltway, I-495, closed due to a spilled grocery truck for an hour. At 0530, second in line. Cold, steady rain but not frozen on the road. Yet an Air Force officer was ahead of me with only a summer-weight blue jacket and a fore and aft cap. I weighed sharing my small pocket umbrella and decided against it. He's a big boy. He should know how to dress himself. After seven minutes, a conversion van pulled up, and the Air Force officer leaped into the shotgun position. As I opened the side sliding door, I asked (for those behind us), "How many?" The driver said, "Five!" Some people take the minimum while others want to help as much as possible on a cold rainy morning. The slug line poured in. I tried to position myself for the early exit but for convenience took the captain's chair behind the driver. Taking on more slugs than required was a good deal for those in line, but it meant cramped quarters for the earlier longer-waiting slugs. The driver was a youngish man, but that's all I could tell. There was some coughing and nose blowing from the back bench seat, but no words were spoken the entire trip. The pile carpeting, extra room and plush seats caused me to luxuriate by laying my running bag, brown bag lunch, Bible, and umbrella on the floor and stretched out. There were two rows of small tree lights, like the emergency evacuation strips on airliners. They gave a low light glow to the cabin. There was a small pillow and card hanging from the rearview mirror. And a large wooden two-cup and music tape holder. Only two tapes were in it. The oldies channel played mellowly on the radio. I opened my eyes occasionally to see what his route was. Occoquan, Lorton, I-95. At one point, I didn't recognize the area and stayed awake long enough to ensure there was nothing to be learned. We took the on-ramp by the auto train in Lorton. Traffic moved well, and there was no rain as I debarked at the bottom of the off ramp at the Pentagon. The radio (at work) reported the outer loop at College Park was (still) closed for the overturned grocery truck.

Going home. I arrived in line at 1530 to help with the extra traffic of a three-day (President's Day Monday) weekend. I got in the right rear of a small sedan, undistinguishable make. Two Army majors were in front, and a South American–looking thin man got in opposite me. The majors were like two cartoon characters. The traffic was normal until approaching Springfield, the mixing bowl. Then rather than take the Springfield bypass, the driver said, "This does not look good!" several times. And his straight man in shotgun agreed each time. Then the driver said, "It's usually not this bad. This is probably the worst we've seen." And shotgun agreed. I began to wonder what we had here. Neophytes. Wet behind the ears. I forced myself to not comment. I really wanted to explode, "You idiots! Take the bypass. What did ya think, it was going to clear up in a mile?" The radio reported a four-car accident near the Occoquan Bridge. Then as we passed the accident, with tow trucks, crushed cars, and damaged railing, the traffic eased up. We only had to go a mile to the Occoquan Bridge, but no, they felt the need to get off the freeway and took the Lorton exit. "At least we'll know where the traffic is, at

Route 123!" shotgun said. Masochists! We managed to avoid easy, free-flowing traffic to queue up in all the lines at the off-ramp. The Lorton, Route 123 line was exceptionally long. I read three-fourth of Acts during the one-and-a-half-hour trek. Mostly with the two majors commenting, "This is bad. This is really bad!" I was glad to get out at Tackett's Mill.

Tuesday, 16 February 1993

One to three inches of snow forecast. Changing to sleet and then rain. Billed as the biggest storm of the season, people parked at the top of hills near their home to get to work. But as I prepared for work, I noted there was no snow. It drizzled on the way to McDonald's at Tackett's Mill. I was fifth in line after the trench coat civilian with dark knit cap covering his head that, on prior occasions, had coughed, hacked, and spit behind the line. Surprisingly, the three of us talked congenially about the weather not being up to its billing. A car took two slugs. Then there was a sound behind us coming from the woods of large raindrops falling. Like a raincloud was moving toward us. We resisted, breaking out our umbrella, playing off the odds of catching a ride first. I broke first as the rain got heavier. A car took the spitter and the black woman. Then a newish four-wheel-drive Jeep XCT took three. I took shotgun, always keeping in mind my exit short of the Pentagon. The driver was an Air Force major. Several things became immediately evident: (1) It was going to be a long, hot drive (my gym bag), with lunch, Bible, and umbrella between my legs. (2) The major was very, very cautious and careful. He took the standard long way down Davis Ford to the now defunct Hechinger's Hardware store. Letting anyone and everyone who felt their time more important to cut in. Lane jumpers were in season. No words were spoken. The radio had garden editor Jack Eden (his real name?) give bulb planting advice. Then the weather situation came on, school closings, and telework authorized for all non-essential personnel, meaning critical personnel only need report to Ft. Meade. Other places had a two-hour delay. Clinton announced his plans for taxing us and reducing the deficit. Ice pellets and snow were round about us. But we got none. Then I asked Mr. Careful to let me out at the bottom of the hill. And he was afraid it would stop traffic. So he took me to the first Pentagon parking lot stop sign, an extra block! If slugs could rate drivers, he would be a zero (0), on a 1–10 scale. A slug's only defense would be to remember and pass the next time in line.

Going home, an older guy in a Toyota van showed up. A woman loaded for the third person as I approached. I waited for a ride. Got a van, and we waited for another slug. Very unusual to wait for both a car and a slug. An older black woman got in back. Driver said he usually picks up five. We talked all the way home about this arrangement. He said he had been doing slug pickups since '85 when he moved to Lakeridge. All kinds of riders, he said. Even one that got in and just slumped and went to sleep.

Wednesday, 17 February 1993

Temperature was thirty-seven degrees with a wind chill of thirteen. Twelfth in line. Everyone stood in slug attention, backs to the wind. Air Force civilian dressed driver with a major in shotgun in a new Camry. They talked promotions all the way in. The captain to my right said they had a board last year and another this to make cuts. Radio on 107.6, Diamond in the Morning, said Clinton's administration changed the word *sacrifice* to "Stick 'em up!" The driver and pax spoke some about the major going to this school or that school. Pride was flowing everywhere, characteristic of all officers, I suppose (having been one).

Going home. Temperature was in the forties, so I took off my trench coat as I stood fifth in line at 1530. I and another slug got into an Oldsmobile with a close-cropped, dark-haired woman driving and an Army colonel in the front right seat. Sometimes uniforms are difficult to make out rank on. And other times, the insignia or rank seem to jump at you. It was that way with the colonel's eagles. They seem to dwarf his uniform as though they were supported to stand out from his uniform shirt. He quickly slumped and slept. No words were spoken the entire route. I read on in Acts in my Bible. The older man on my right broke out a library book and stayed in it. His heavy breathing caused me to look to see if he was asleep. He wasn't.

Thursday, 18 February 1993

Running late, I eliminated all unnecessary movement as I was up late for a small-group church meeting at our house, not for Clinton's (Bill) economic speech. Surprisingly, I found myself caught up, eighth in line at 0530. It was cold (three degrees with wind chill). An Air Force captain and I were soon picked up in a Honda that was cramped in back. I could hardly get in behind the driver, a blond close-cut Air Force captain. An Air Force major with dark hair sat to his right. They talked continuously, but it was barely audible in the back with road noise and rear speakers. I had to hold my gym bag with lunch in my lap. The driver made no attempt to move his seat; slugs have no rights. I observed his initial driving before dozing on I-95. He stayed left lane until near the now defunct Hechinger's, then tried to cut right, back into the right turn lane. When the car to his right didn't relinquish immediately, he said, "Jerk," and sped up to slide in. I could only imagine what the driver of the other car was saying. On ramp to I-95, he didn't continue sliding left but came to a somewhat alarming stop in the right lane. He did the Pentagon off-ramp very pronounced, pulling forward and right to drop me off. I felt cold on my ankles as I walked under the I-95 overpass near the Pentagon and through the parking lot, empty except for one police car, through the Doubletree Hotel overhang with two vans loading airplane pilots and flight attendants, many in red suit coats. I have noticed through my commute and running at lunchtime these flight crews get paid a set amount to stay overnight and so work up the least-expensive motel deal they can get and keep the change. A group of us lunch runners would get one hotel or another to let us shower in a used room before it had been cleaned for like $10 each a month. Often flight crews were checking out or in even in the cheapest of

Crystal City hotels, right next to Reagan International Airport. I arrived at work at 0611. I worked the cypher lock and opened the door. The security alarm sounded as I had forgotten the security key. I quickly turned it off and reopened the door. Nice!

Going home. Clear and cold, second in line, only the Oriental woman with pink ear muffs ahead of me. She wasn't in the right position to be in either the Potomac Mills or Tackett's Mill pickup lines. So I asked her which line she was in, me wondering if I could have to wait in a car for another slug. She said, "No, I'm going to Ames." I told her no one goes there, and she replied, "I usually ride from the district, but today I'm over here." Whatever. After a considerably cold wait, the mother of a boys' soccer team player picked up the three of us. I sat in front, and we discussed the baseball and football her boys were in, which interested me for my son, who plays only soccer. A woman about my age sat behind me, and an Air Force officer was in left rear, but neither spoke the entire trip. The mother's son called on her cell phone approaching Backlick Road exit, and she gave a position report. I knew she was divorced and had three children. Must be tough. She told me about her volunteering to be a football assistant coach. The head coach said they were looking for a man to help but could give no reason why a woman couldn't do it. They finally said she could if she could pass a football test, which no one else had to take. Whoa! When the sports ran out, the conversation ended. I was disappointed. I didn't get to read the Bible in my gym bag.

Friday, 19 February 1993

Twelve degrees with a wind chill to negative-seventeen degrees! Third in line. We joked about it not getting any better, weather-wise, and theorized about more drivers. Trench coat, knit cap, gloves, suit, underclothes, and I felt naked. It was so cold. My face hurt standing there. After five minutes, as the Air Force officer theorizes, a former slug, driving because it was so cold, picked us up. The Bronco XLT with awkward-moving front seat. The heavyset black woman with a shawl and officer got in back. I took shotgun. Xtra 107 played oldies as the heater became felt. No words were spoken all the way in. A green Christmas tree freshener swung from the rearview mirror. Traffic moved well, likely from people not coming in. I passed two airline crew buses loading as I passed the Doubletree Hotel and was taking off my coat in the office at 0605.

Monday, 22 February 1993

I went to bed with a great deal of trepidation for today. Snow had turned to freezing rain and sleet, and it stayed in the cul-de-sac as a sheet of ice. A friend had asked for a ride (he usually walked) to the slug line as he was going on travel and had luggage. Temperature was about thirty-four degrees, allowing some areas of ice and snow to melt. The morning sounds were mostly draining water. I threw boots in the back, my running bag (it was supposed to reach fifty degrees today), lunch, and attaché brief. I left at 0505 to arrive at my friend's house one and a half miles away by 0520. He had a friend with luggage also to pick up. I found it icy and slippery in our neighborhood streets, but there were ruts down to the pavement. It turned out to be easygoing, and I arrived at his house at 0510 and waited. The alternative plan was to take a bus from the shopping center across the street (Dillingham Square). He opened the door and waved at 0515. Radio had only one school delay as I listened and waited. I helped him with his luggage, and his friend, paranoid at being a slug, bailed out. The main roads were dry although it was very foggy out. My brake caution light came on and beamed red brightly. Need brake fluid. We arrived in the slug line at 0530, and my friend caught the third car, allowing us to talk for a few minutes. The very next car asked for a Crystal City rider. Most of us had given up asking since the preponderance was Pentagon or State Department, and I got in behind a Navy lieutenant commander driver and Air Force major. It was a newish Honda. There were other bags in the back, and the lieutenant commander's uniform jacket was hanging up. They discussed the major's trip Saturday to see the Vatican's display at the Congressional Library. Letters from King George to the Pope supporting the church but explaining his position on Martin Luther. And documents showing attendance of the Sistine Chapel choir. The major went to Murphy's in Old Town, Alexandria, and he hosted his brother and wife and another brother to the tune of a $150 bar tab. His single brother met a woman who showed him around DC Sunday. He asked how the lieutenant commander's weekend was, and he went into detail on Tricare tax. They kept this up all the way to Crystal City. They were going to Crystal Gateway 3, my building! I stayed dry to the parking lot and was at work by 0610.I needed a miracle to get to work in the snow and slush this morning, and I got it.

Going home. The day had turned balmy, with temperatures in the low fifties. As I approached the slug line at the Pentagon, it was unreal. The Potomac Mills line was well down the bus island, probably forty to fifty people. The Tackett's Mill line was some twenty people long. And we waited and waited. It was as though a strike was in force against picking up slugs. Typically, a small car or four-door sedan would take two; the vans and minivans, one or two. I was about tenth in line when the Toyota van of a work-all-night guy pulled up and took five! Finally, I was third, and a canary yellow Ford station wagon rattled itself in front of us. An Air Force officer and a woman got in back. I took shotgun; many riders just wanted to sleep through the trip and not be engaged in talking, which the shotgun position often implied, talking with the driver. The station wagon was driven by a middle-aged man in a dark-blue parka, not seemingly dressed for Washington office work. Maybe blue-collar worker. Wore glasses and was sort of heavyset. Looked very like my father-in-law. He and I exchanged comments on being glad to finally catch a ride. And then silence for the duration. I didn't see a radio, and neither did he turn one on. Traffic was building as we approached the Lorton exit. I looked through my bills folders as we stop and crawled. The car seemed barely able to hold together. It rattled and made ready-to-fall-apart noises from every part of the car. It chugged and wheezed as blue collar put the gear shift through its motions. We finally had to move from the HOV lane to the right as a sporty TR3 had collided with the rear of a full-sized van. Both were dented but no serious harm. A Good Samaritan van was behind the TR3 and a police car with rotators going behind it. The slowdown was primarily rubbernecking. He stopped at McDonald's, close to my car, and we all thanked him and bailed out.

Tuesday, 23 February 1993

Fifth in line at 0525. About twenty degrees, with wind chill to ten. Amazingly, the canary yellow station wagon with butterscotch interior clattered and chugged to a stop. An Air Force colonel took shotgun, a hooded woman took right rear, and I took left rear seats. The driver had given no sign how many slugs he would take or where he was headed. I should mention here that some drivers took no more than the minimum, two riders to make HOV-3, because more weight used more gas and cost more. Other drivers took as many as they could, out of sympathy, not giving priority to some small increase in gas cost. I guess there is another consideration for possible injury from accidents.

It was very cold in his car, like stepping out of a refrigerator into a walk-in freezer. He must live nearby. No words were spoken. None. No radio. All the vibrations, rattles, and impending break-down noises seemed very loud. I had seen the hooded woman in the slug line before but short with long brown hair. She kept her hood up, I noticed, out of my peripheral vision, as if she had leprosy and was hiding it. I finally broke the rattle-filled silence with my request to be dropped at the bottom of the Pentagon off-ramp. He said, "No, I won't!" Then he laughed. Wow! No communication whatso-ever and then abrupt humor! I joked back, "Okay, I'll jump out here [on the off-ramp]." He let me out at the traffic light since we were stopped anyway.

Going home. It was very cold and windy. Probably wind chill to ten degrees or so. Twenty people in line at 1530! Finally, at 1600, I and a heavily bundled black woman got in a small sedan with an Air Force officer. She sat in front and could hear the Pat and Mike radio show which apparently was funny as they laughed periodically.

I only caught snippets. So I settled in and finished Acts in my Bible. I had forgotten Paul went through such a sailing ordeal getting to Rome for trial.

Wednesday, 24 February 1993

It was 0525, very cold. So cold, many slugs (there were about twenty in line) faced the woods, putting the wind at our backs. The trench coat spitter got in line to my left, spitting. We began talking though and thoroughly discussed the unexpectedness of slug transportation. He and I finally got a small two-door car, not a slug's favorite because of the difficulty getting in, besides being small inside. I told him I needed the door for my exit at the Pentagon off-ramp. So he attempted to get in back. The young woman driver with unprepared straight dark hair could offer no help. He and I felt for knobs and handles with no success. He was to the left, and I on the right. He said just move the seat up. I couldn't tell if the handle moved up or back and forth. It released, and the seat moved forward, still not far enough to let him in. We continued to feel around the seat as the slugs behind us laughed. I heard the comment, "It's been a long time since we had this kind of entertainment!" I turned and said, "I had $5 on the monkey." More laughter. Somehow, the seat tripped, tilted forward, and he got in. More fumbling to get the seat back. As I got the door closed and we got going, the woman driver apologized and said she normally slugs at 0730, and there is no line. In four years, it's been no problem. Arriving that late, I could see parking as the biggest difficulty. She said traffic was lighter at 0730 to 0800 also. If only I could do that and go home at 1530 too! She and I talked all the way in. The spitter slug went to EMCOM Alpha, total silence. She and her husband had bought a Fredericksburg home. He would commute to Belvoir while she trained all the way to Pentagon City. The builders were to lay the foundation this week but hadn't yet. They expected a coordination problem as they sold their house and were to be out in April. She said the builders, Battlefield Homes, were very nice, and the neighbors down there were great. I told her we almost moved to Falmouth, expecting the Virginia Railway Express (VRE) to come available soon. Our teenaged daughter said all the kids swore continuously at high school, so we wanted to get the kids into a Christian school to protect them and provide a more relaxed pace of life.

Friday, 26 February 1993

Snow as forecast! About one inch on the ground. The still-falling snow looked very peculiar, like falling glitter. Hardly any cars in the McDonald's lot. I was the only car in the lane adjacent to the drive-through. I parked directly in front of the drive-through window to facilitate their watching my car. No one in the slug line. An Air Force colonel, his eagles bright on the dark-blue uniform, crossed ahead of me, and we noted two or three cleared spots in the slug line snow, as if some previous slugs had been beamed up. Although the radio had said the wind chill temperature was twelve degrees, it was relatively pleasant standing there in the snow. Little wind. Another Air Force officer came up and said he was new in the area and asked if the buses would run today. The colonel and I looked at each other as though wondering what made us the commuter bus transit authority. No, we felt the bus was a sure thing. The colonel explained we were the slug line and the bus line forms over there with the shelter. He went for the bus stop.

We then got picked up by a new van. The colonel went first, climbing in the back with instruction to "push everything over." I got in the middle, with the car seat. The seat belt pulled from the left, so I guessed it was a Toyota. An enlisted young guy in Army green fatigues sat in front of me. The driver was . . . the cautious guy or girl I had ridden with before. He or she reminded me of James Bowie of movie fame. High cheekbones, short hair for a girl, long for a guy. He or she appeared to be in an Air Force uniform. He or she sat well forward, gripping the wheel with both hands. The road had always previously rejected the snow, melting it. Today the road seemed to accept and hold the snow, making even this light snowfall treacherous to drive. Traffic moved fairly well to Springfield, where a police car's twirling blue light behind an abandoned car slowed traffic. A killer tractor trailer truck kept pace with us, two lanes over to the right up to the segregated HOV lanes. There was no talking, only the loud twang of country music: "My hands were sweaty, my knees were shaking, love's got a hold on me" and "She held on to the rock, in the storm." It was a good day to have a cautious driver. She or he dropped me at the light at the bottom of the Pentagon off-ramp.

Monday, 1 March 1993

Very cold. About ten degrees, but no wind. The snow and water from the previous day were frozen rocks. The roads were clear, and I parked quickly next to the waiting truck in front of the McDonald's window. I was fifth in line at 0530. Spitter lined up to my left; a smallish, thin Air Force captain was on my right. One car came and picked up two. The "in your face" guy crossed directly in front of the twenty-plus-long line. He had on a black Russian-style hat, brown coat with turned-up collar, and hands in pockets. A cardboard sign gave the number of a Navy commander that had slug's leather gloves. The next car was large and luxurious. One guy made no effort to ask if two could go. I was fourth in line and could make the next car if he went in the plainly roomy, large car. I spoke up, "Take two?" The shotgun passenger with coffee cup rolled his window down and said, "Yes, two, I'm sorry!" The lead guy scrambled to get in. The captain and I got in a new Camry. Another benefit of slugging is getting to ride in every make and model of car for your own evaluation. The driver said, "Buckle up, please!" And I knew I was with the major and the civilian, as he (the major) always asked. The captain immediately went to sleep mode while the driver today with a gray sweatshirt and the major discussed things at work. I caught only snippets as the sound speaker volume was up in back, on 107.3, Diamond in the Morning radio show. News was of the New York World Trade Towers attack. One organization called before the blast, and seventeen wanted credit afterward. A religious battle was going on between authorities and a man claiming to be Jesus. "Jesus" apparently had taken hostages, and there was shooting, several people dead. Also, the airlift to Croatia had been a success. I got out at the bottom of the hill, the driver very skillfully swinging wide to let me out safely. I was at work by 0610.

Going home. A brief line, two or three people, moved quickly, and I got in the back of the OWL Volunteer Fire Department SUV. "How did you guess?" he asked as there was a yellow beacon mounted on the dashboard. A middle-aged black woman got in shotgun. It was only a two-door small car. The kind slugs prefer not to get in, but will. There was no discussion. I wrapped myself up in Joshua, a book of the Bible I wasn't very familiar with. Wow! God parted the Jordan River, too, for the Israelites. That parting of the waters doesn't get as much press like the Red Sea. Achan, an Israelite, kept some of the plunder from their God-given conquests as all the people east of the Jordan had "melted hearts" from fear of the Israelis. An expected victory at Ai turned to a route for their enemies, and Joshua asked why. They asked each tribe and each person one by one until Achan revealed his coveted clothing and silver. So Joshua had the people take him, his sons, daughters, belongings, and animals, and stoned him. Then the Lord gave Joshua the strategy to route Ai.

Tuesday, 2 March 1993

Weather forecast of fifty-five degrees today brought out fair-weather slugs in force. I was tenth in line at 0525, next to a middle-aged black woman I wasn't familiar with. Spitter lined up to my left. There was no line movement, and soon the line was thirty or so long, heading for Burger King around the corner. I found myself talking with both the black woman and spitter, she about when the cars come (she normally left at 0730) and he about the people in line. He occasionally chortled, sniffing up his sinus drain. He finally turned to his left and spit. Cars were picking up one at a time. A guy at the head of the line was turning down rides, waiting for a Crystal City ride. He said he had to go to the south end that he normally caught metro at the Pentagon. I told him he could walk, with most of it in the Crystal City underground, but he was aware of it already. The black woman got a big car with a shirt hanging up in the rear window, our side. A huge Chevy truck with a pinched front pulled up, and I kidded spitter this guy would take five. He took me and that with difficulty. Shotgun guy had to stand up and pull the seat forward. The bench seat was okay, but there was no connection with the cavern behind us. I resisted the temptation to ask if he carried horses. Driver was an Air Force major, and his shotgun friend in a red starter-like windbreaker was an Air Force officer in disguise (close haircut and glasses). They talked continuously as we surprisingly took the Occoquan cut through Lorton and on to I-95 by the auto-train (which carries cars to Florida). His truck felt too big for the narrow Occoquan Road. Hell, it felt too big for I-95! The radio droned in the background as they discussed the World Trade tower bombing. I had mentioned there was three days of rain coming Wednesday to Friday and then entered slug reticence. Shotgun mentioned a class with an FBI agent, and he bragged on the terrorist squads. He said they had sharpshooters that spend half their day practicing accuracy, using a shooter's alley, hitting the head portion without fail. And he related a hostage incident in which the bad guy turned his head and they picked him off. I dismounted, with difficulty, the truck, taking most to the Pentagon road.

Going home. Fifty-five degrees balmy. Twenty-plus people in line. The line hadn't doubled back yet, but I was near the Dale City bus shelter. Why? Yesterday it was a five-minute wait. Today it would be fifteen minutes. There was lots of consternation as people asked if this was the Tackett's Mill line, incredulous it was not the Dale City line. An Army H-1 helicopter in dark camouflage colors flew low, very low, from the Pentagon river side south to the helipad on the west side, directly over us. It set off numerous car security alarms. They whooped and beeped in chorus. Funny. Slugs are always looking for entertainment in line. Got in a 1993 brand-new car with a woman in her forties driving. She had reddish straight shoulder-length hair and a black-and-white half sweater blouse. The fat Navy chief in the front right talked with briefly about what kind of car it was, but it still smelled new. There were buttons all over the center of the steering wheel where the air bag would have been, had there been one. I joked with them, "I guess there's no air bag!" There were other gadgets and gizmos, buttons, and whatnots over the dash. Passengers had electric windows and ashtrays. It wasn't very roomy in back, but I had it all to myself. The chief pulled a book out to read, and I got out my Bible to read Joshua. Wow! The Israelites won victory after victory. Joshua even prayed and had God stop the sun in place so they could have sufficient time to route their enemy. The book ended anticlimactic as details of land allocation were related.

Wednesday, 3 March 1993

Twelfth in line at 0525! Fairly nice out. I had my leather attaché and lunch, trench coat open, umbrella in pocket for expected rain this afternoon. Saw the canary yellow station wagon take three. Slugs joked about it rattling along. I still remember it had 139,000 miles. I missed a ride in a small two-door car, then got a new two-door sport car. I told the chief getting in with me I needed the door for a bottom of the hill exit at the Pentagon. He let me in front, and I got in so quickly I caught his leg with the seat flopping back. Damn, toy sports car! I was cramped with my attaché brief. The driver was an older man, suffering midlife crisis. This was his toy. He played heavy rock on DC 101 and sipped from a mug held in the center console. The flip-up headlights presented a non-geometric shape behind their light. We made a few comments about the weather then listened to the radio all the way in. He turned right and dropped me at the light.

Going home. Approaching the slug line from the east, I was held up by two cars, one after the other. As I approached the line, an Army officer sped up from the opposite direction. We arrived very nearly at the same time, and I edged ahead. Miffed, he was rushing to set me back. We talked about line length awhile and then waited. Slugs are aware that being one person back in line may turn into a long wait between pickups. As it turned out, we still waited about ten to fifteen minutes in line. A new Saturn finally took us. I didn't see his rank, the Army uniform being resplendent with numerous adornments. He had a larger nose than mine and was rather outspoken. He got in back as I assumed shotgun. The driver was a middle-aged woman in an all-black dress. The three of us talked all the way home about new cars and the Army officer had bought an Aerostar for towing a new trailer, Sunbeam, I think. He whipped out a brochure. Said he had three boys—four, two, and some months—and they loved to go places. The driver was well pleased with the attention the Saturn dealer gave her, checking weekly to see if all was okay. She said she only had one complaint, the tachometer and speedometer should be reversed, with the tachometer on the left. Army man tried to justify as reading direction. She had been in the Army, and both she and her Army husband had enough camping exercises. Army man got in Desert Storm had been enough, but the kids liked camping. Camping with a van? Guess this was a compromise. Anyway, she was now a VA adjudicator and launched into a litany of complicated state, federal, and individual complications as we sat in the longest line at Lorton I had ever seen. We barely got on the crossroad. Non-HOV traffic had been heavy, but we never heard an accident on the radio, which was tuned very low in volume.

Thursday, 4 March 1993

Raining hard with 25–30 mph winds. One of the worst weather days yet. I was behind the truck parker guy pulling into the Tackett's Mill parking lot. He had cut me off coming down the road, and I had used my high-beam headlights in protest. As he maneuvered to back in, I whipped into a vacant spot and hustled to the line. As I crossed the street, a short Spanish-descent man in a trench coat was virtually running to beat me to fifth in line. I chuckled as I crossed the street. I could have beat him, and sometimes, one person makes a big difference. Today it didn't. His cloth trench coat belt had trailed him in the sidewalk puddles as he rushed to beat me. I told him his thing was trailing, and he tucked it away. He had a mustache and glasses. I didn't want this guy to get a car ahead of me. Principle of the thing.

We waited fifteen minutes in a heavy, cold, rain. Fortunately there was no wind. Finally the canary yellow jalopy station wagon took three, and a new minivan took three. I got in perfect egress position, last, by the sliding door. A small black woman was in front right, and the Spaniard was on my left. The driver was an officer, but I didn't try to make out the uniform or rank. The seat belt was already connected and fastened on the right. I strapped in and felt my feet restricted. The Spaniard had left his brief toward my side. I pushed it over with my feet. He could put it under his legs. My pants legs were soaked so that I was wet and cold. The driver, however, never turned the heat on. The van had two little enclaves for passengers up front, with an instrumented console in the middle. I guess he was trying not to fog up the windows, but it was as cold as an icebox. He had a dark military jacket on and drove very slow. We were cut off numerous times, most obnoxiously down Davis Ford and approaching the on ramp to I-95. Usually, single drivers, but why are they more important than an HOV-loaded car? The radio had Jack Eden, garden editor, speak on two storms last week and losing branches from snow. He gets paid for this? News of the day followed: The Waco cult leader, David Koreesh, was still a holdout, a California man burst into a house claiming he was Christ, and the airlift to Bosnia was successful according to aircrews, although reports said supplies were not dropped where they could be picked up. The wind turned my umbrella inside out as I fought to walk to the office. I released the catch and let the umbrella be flexible, holding it into the wind to come back into proper form. I cut through the Double Tree Hotel overhangs to the Crystal City underground to work.

Going home. The storm was still with us—30 mph winds, pouring rain, twenty-seven-degree wind chill. Very uncomfortable walking to the Pentagon. Eighth in line. Three were picked up as I arrived. Ahead of me were three officers. One was an Air Force major with only a jacket and fore and aft cap. Another was an Army major, beet red from the cold blowing rain. Rain dripped from his unprotected face and nose. And there was a very tall Army colonel holding a small newspaper up to the wind. He turned and said it was an Army umbrella! Nuts! The uniform designers didn't provide sound foul weather clothes. And I knew from being a Navy officer we weren't expected to carry umbrellas as it might prevent you from saluting when you needed to. These observations were made while struggling to keep my already-bent folding umbrella from being turned inside out. It did several times over fifteen minutes before a Camry picked me and the guy behind me up. I got in shotgun, and the other guy, behind me. An Air Force major was driving. Regular car lanes were stopped the entire HOV. What didn't seem fair was that whenever the regular traffic lanes had an accident, the people in charge would open up the HOV lanes to relieve the traffic, essentially punishing those of us abiding by the HOV rules. I finished Joshua and started Judges as the driver occasionally alerted us to road incidents. A stopped pickup in the regular lanes. Pump and maintenance crews were pumping water out of the center overflowing ditch. Afterward, it was clear sailing.

Friday, 5 March 1993

Cloudy, cold (about twenty-seven degrees), little wind. There was a flail in the lot as several cars maneuvered to back into parking. This obnoxious dance of the elephants was bypassed, and I made sixth in line. Our breath was clearly visible, rising and drifting right. It's a real surprise to see how much of someone else's already-breathed air we breathe. A large pickup in the McDonald's lot was parked, motor running, parking lights on. The driver was shaving with an electric shaver. At least twenty of us slugs watched as he continued. Then when a car pulled into the drive-through, he looked in the rearview mirror to see how he did. A minivan took three. A smaller car pulled up; the Navy captain to my right took shotgun. I got in back right, and the tall, thin trench-coated man to my left asked, "Three?" I didn't want him as the car wasn't that big. The driver, a blond, clean-cut, bespectacled Air Force captain (two bars), said, "Yes!" I had to put my gym bag and lunch bag in my lap. There was no room at my feet. The tall, thin guy then pulled out a handheld light and a large library book and read Pacific War history. There was no discussion. The driver played the radio, switching several times. The New York World Trade Center suspect, Mohammed Salami, was arrested when he went to claim money for a stolen rental van. The radio faded until I could barely hear it even with the rear speaker behind me. I did hear the Waco, Texas, holding out to God, waiting for Him to direct them. As I cut through the Doubletree Hotel overhang, I saw a trash can with at least three bent and twisted umbrellas, victims of yesterday's rain and high winds. Many homes, schools, and businesses are still without power. More umbrella carcasses were strewn about Crystal City on the walk to work.

Monday, 8 March 1993

At 0525, I crossed the street on a dry, cloudy, cool morning (forty-five degrees), and for some reason, I was only fifteenth in line! Also unusual, though, was that pickups began early, at 0535. I lined up next to a short, plump, middle-aged white woman in a trench coat. Spitter soon joined to my left (remember, we slugs face the street). He said hi and laughed at the line length. We discussed why this should be so, and soon the short woman jumped into the discussion, encouraged by our talking. But I knew spitter. He was a slug trooper; I didn't know her. She mentioned cars can hardly see the dark uniforms as we observed cars coming and going to the McDonald's lot. One car turned wide to avoid a walking officer and practically hit the curb. Spitter sounded over his cold, yet he turned and spit for no apparent reason. The canary wagon picked up three; it was very dirty and had a new ticking noise to accompany all the other sounds of deterioration. As we talked, In-Your-Face made a two-third line run. He had a shorter jacket in place of his long winter coat and no hat. He still acted like we, the slugs, were not heel to the eastern sidewalk edge. The short woman and I completed a threesome pickup in a small four-door car. I got in back left. It was the close-cut blond Air Force captain! His season for me, I guess. A major of Air Force or Army origin was front right. The radio was on WTOP and stayed there. No discussion this trip. He pulled his usual down the left until near the now defunct Hechinger's when he jumped lanes to the right. Jerk! I felt like a spy in the enemy's camp. Should I use piano wire and strangle him? Or bring the intelligence back for a strike? There were no obstructions to travel, and I arrived at work at 0610.

Tuesday, 9 March 1993

Forecast overnight thunderstorm never materialized. It was partly cloudy, with a full moon. And still quite cold. I was eighth in line at the same arrival time as yesterday—0525, fifteenth to eighth! Who can figure? I queued up to spitter, and we began slug line and weather discussions. His daughter and son-in-law had driven through Ohio and Breezewood, going into and out of snow. He then inhaled through his nose to draw the drainage down and spit to his right behind him. A few moments of silence as Strategic Air Command (SAC) man, with short leather jacket collar, was on my left. I think most Air Force guys join just for the leather SAC jacket, SAC members or not. We have leather flight jackets in the Navy, too, but it cannot be worn off base, since it is a piece of flight gear. A car asked for two. Another for Crystal City. A guy ahead of me and myself stepped forward. I got in right rear, he in shotgun. As gray, wild-haired Dorothy started forward, two pedestrians stopped, started, stopped as Dorothy did the same with her car. Another guy approached her left front while this bunching was occurring. She commented people are hard to see at night. All of them finally crossed in front of her. And as I completed buckling up, I became aware of Arctic outside air pouring in. The front right window was down, and the guy sitting there was groping for the window controls. He looked to Dorothy, and she said, "Oh, is the window plunged?" and electrically raised it. As she turned onto Davis Ford to the right, she commented (I don't know what prompted it) she once took a girl to Crystal City and she didn't know where she was to go. She was used only to the underground. After driving her around, Dorothy finally dropped her to fend for herself. We then entered the silence as though we were about to undergo a transformation process. We listened to an oldies radio channel, with mellow '60s music (my high school generation) going in. As Doro passed the stop light, a guy zoomed from her right to a left turn in front of her into the Doubletree driveway. She got confused, started to turn, and then corrected herself. "Was confused there a moment by him turning." Remarkably she had just been abused by a driver and didn't even realize it. She dropped me in the median in front of Crystal Gateway 3.

Going home. I was seventh or eighth. The guy that drives a dirty four-door Nissan Sentra covered with bird droppings pulled up on the left, took a woman out of order, and went to wait at the close in bus stop for his wife. I and two others got a middle-aged woman in a Honda, four-door. Music played but there was no discussion, just the sound of the driver up and down shifting.

Wednesday, 10 March 1993

Still very cold. Could almost see your breath. The waning full moon was behind a hazy cloud cover. Even though I was again in line at 0525, I was sixteenth in line. What the heck is going on? After a ten-minute wait, British Dorothy pulled up, but three Crystal City people forward of me took the ride. Then the blonde crew-cut Air Force captain pulled up. Then the rattling canary wagon. An Air Force captain was on my right with a cake pan covered in foil. He had no gloves, and the pan, I'm certain, was a cold sink. He periodically set it on the sidewalk. The stocky woman to my left was familiar, in a turquoise coat and a haircut that reminded me of Elvis Presley. Her dark hair was long in back and swept back on the sides. To her immediate left was the heavyset black woman with the shawl wrapped around her neck. As the Air Force captain and I took one and two respectively, I joked with him we needed to complain to the driver's union and get the drivers rescheduled. He agreed they needed to do better. I mentioned that pan must be really cold. He said, "Yeah, it's amazing what we bring to work and how we get there. Other people just wouldn't understand this, and I can't believe I'm doing it!"

Finally, a van with seat belt buckles on the left. I couldn't tell from inside, but after I got out, I saw a Chevy emblem. Anyway, the center bench seat was out. I told Elvis woman I needed the door for early exit, and she took left rear. I took right rear and could not find the seat belt. I own a minivan, so I knew to feel for it behind and under the seat. Nothing. I repeatedly felt for it in every conceivable location. Nothing. I asked the driver, "You got a seat belt back here?" He said, "Yes, last time I looked." Elvis tried to help, but there was no belt. I fussed around for about ten minutes and finally resigned my fate to an accident-free ride, with the middle seat out and no belt! I felt I was on a catapult, waiting for launch. We got to the right-turn traffic light okay, but the bespeckled, jacketed driver felt the curb by the light too dangerous, and he drove another block to pull in the parking lot. I thanked him although I wanted to curse him. Next time, I'll walk from Tackett's Mill!

Going home, I raced a tall, thin civilian to the line. Remembered the last guy that overtook me and left me ten minutes longer in line. This time, I had the angle and won the race. Tenth or so in line at 1530! Weather was cool and cloudy. A haze-gray H-3 helicopter marked HC-2 flew low over us, the pilots side-slipping rather than coordinating a turn to the helipad (pre-911, the pad was on the west side of the Pentagon.) There was one Navy, one Army, and most of the rest Air Force officers ahead. The Air Force let out routinely like they were all in the same class or something. I and another young civilian guy finally got a small two-door car with a very young thin man driving. He pulled forward to the Potomac Mills line, backed to the bus shelter, and then to in front of us. He said he was new at this as we got in. The whole slug line saw his indecision, an anomaly in slug procedures. The other guy climbed in back, and as I crowded into the front seat, I looked back at the slug line and said, "Quick, take the license number!" They laughed (eight to ten people), and one woman said, "No, you're on your own now." I replied, "Wait a minute, we're all in this together." The door closing belted me automatically. As I took the lap belt, the driver asked where to go next. I provided direction all the way to Tackett's Mill. He said he lived at Lake of the Woods in Fredericksburg and was trying to work out a new way to get home. A friend had mentioned slugs, but little did he know how far from I-95 he would have to go. He mentioned the Ames slugs, but I told him I don't know where they line up to go home. As we got out at McDonald's, I told the other slug, "That's the last we'll see of him!"

Thursday, 11 March 1993

Cool, forty-five degrees, partly cloudy and the moon bright in the breaks. Fifteenth in line again. I lined up next to spitter. He said he missed yesterday, as though I was his boss, and he was explaining his absence. Otherwise, we would have lined up next to each other three or four days in a row. As previously mentioned, it was typical to have "seasons" or periods of lining up with or riding with the same slugs and/or drivers for a period of time. Said he took his daughter and son-in-law to the monuments and museums. Washington Monument had almost no line. I told him I went to the University of Illinois, and he said, "Yeah, I know where that is." We bantered about the line getting longer with good weather as we noted a bird chirping and agreed spring was coming. (It would snow Friday and Saturday.) Dorothy pulled up, and yesterday's scenario repeated itself. Three guys forward of me got in. If I could just beat them in the morning.

Going home. About the normal, routine slug process. Getting in and not talking, or as the other slug Mrs. Robinson stated, "Getting in and not allowing anyone else to talk, by radio, by silence, or by dominating talking yourself." The car was a four-door sedan and of comfortable size. One of the many benefits of slugging is you experience every make and model of car to form your own opinion of what to buy next. You might give up a two-door economy car for a four-door sedan if you knew you might be driving slugs occasionally so as to not socially embarrass yourself. As slugs entered the two-door type you could sense the feeling of loss of control and having to do more with less, again, for the cost free ride and being able to save time. I pulled out company health-care forms to read, and Mrs. Robinson dozed. We bantered some when a single driver suddenly got in front of us after Springfield. On being dropped off, the driver and she walked over to the Tackett's Mill Safeway together.

Friday, 12 March 1993

Arrived eighth in line. An experienced slug stood explaining to his friend how the system worked. Swell! A slug recruit for more ride competition. Few slugs today, probably more because others had the compressed work schedule (CWS)—government and military have acronyms for everything—Friday off. The concept is the government employee works four 10-hour days and then gets Friday off, saving one commute. Some take Monday off. Either way, the reduction in cars on the road is noticeable as well as the reduction in slug rides. I was hoping for Dorothy from NAVSEA for a ride to be dropped off at my door in Crystal City. Instead, I got the aging van with captain chairs. The civilian driver took five slugs. I took left rear, and the new guy got the captain chair by the door. A popsicle stick with small pillow swung from the rearview mirror. Two rows of strip slights on the ceiling led to the overhead window and illuminate the room softly. Oldies miscellaneous music in the background. Kitchen sink in the back! Soft light from the console around two tapes.

Going home. Tenth in line. I got there early at 1525! The snow storm of the decade was forecast to begin this afternoon and continue through Saturday. That was enough to keep many government employees (the ones that weren't already off for CWS) from coming to work. I got into a big blue Dodge Ram truck. A medical-like snake and staff silver emblem hung from the rearview mirror on a chain. Only it was dragon wings with an evil-looking snake. The chief asked what it meant, and the driver said he didn't know. I doubt it. I slid into the window seat with, it turned out, a submarine chief or senior chief. I had been in cars with him before, and he talked incessantly. Today was no different. Probably to make up for all that isolation underwater was my guess. The civilian driver was the stout or chunky guy that looked a lot like my father-in-law. He had been a jet mechanic when he took nine months of computer courses and now could "strip computers to parade rest and put them back together." The chief was very interested as he was getting out soon. Seems there is a Nouvelle qual tech and a Banyun qual. He had the Banyun, which included Nouvelle software. "How much do you get paid?" the chief asked. "Fifty to fifty-four thousand dollars after you get established, which takes five to eight years."

The usual Friday traffic slowed to a snail's pace at Newington on the HOV side, while the right two lanes zoomed by. The driver was so taken by someone interested in his work he forgot he was driving. Pop music played in the background. I think he would have changed to the right lane if he had paid attention to his surroundings. He gesticulated many points, taking his hands off the wheel. The chief responded enthusiastically, occasionally turning to me with a "Know what I mean?" and "How about you?" After we discussed where we worked, I fell out of the conversation. I was an officer, and they were enlisted. They talked about Great Lakes as a boot camp and how bad it was. The chief mentioned base closures would move NAVSEA to White Oakes, Maryland, and NAVAIR to Patuxent River. The chief's language was full of expletives, foul language learned through many days at sea, I guess.

Monday, 15 March 1993

Walked three miles from our house to the Tackett's Mill slug line. I was going to catch the bus, but when I walked to the Weis shopping center, there was no sign of life and I have no patience. Plus I didn't know for certain the bus wasn't cancelled. It was so cold. My fingers in my gloves were painfully cold, and I periodically pulled them into the warmth of my palms. I had my gym bag with shoes, *Lord of the Flies* paperback, and lunch. I walked opposite traffic in the dry street except when cars came. The snow was rock hard, frozen, and crunchy. I bought bagel knots and then immediately caught a Navy captain in a newish Volvo. A Navy lieutenant got in back, never said a word. Intimidated, I'd guessed. The captain and I discussed the road conditions. He had gotten out to scrape the windshield when we got in. Gradually, his windshield became covered with dirty snow, but he never used the washer fluid. Probably out. There was a line getting onto the HOV lanes at Springfield, and I would have stayed in regular traffic. It was obvious the road crews had not plowed the HOV. There was a long line at the off-ramp. Normally, two lanes was one due to snow and ice. I read *Lord of the Flies* while we bumped over hard ice and spread dirt. The captain's ship cup was hot, and the steam, as it was jammed in the dash, was frozen to the windshield. The streets and sidewalks were all ice. I gingerly picked my way to work, arriving at 0700, a one and a half hour commute that is normally thirty minutes.

Going home, I was wearing boots, knit cap, and all. Walked through snow and ever-so-icy boulder-strewn landscape. Eighth in line, I discussed the frozen snow with a guy I had seen many times. He mentioned his difficulty in getting to the line, and I replied I had walked three miles this morning. Remarkably, he passed up a ride so that we could go together in the same car to talk some more. He was picking up his daughter and then driving to the Weis shopping center for ravioli. Remarkable! God's grace! The odds of this happening, if at all, are astronomical. You'd have a better chance of winning the lottery. I didn't have to walk the three miles home. The blisters on my heel could rest. He took me to Cricket Lane, the street that had been plowed close to my house. His four-year-old, Kathy, was already working his 386 computer.

Tuesday, 16 March 1993

Slipped into a slot next to the idling pickup with waiting driver. Made about tenth in line. The frozen snow and ice extended across the sidewalk and out for half a car lane, as though slug beach had enlarged for low tide. I didn't put my knit cap on, and my ears got painfully cold. My right foot also was freezing. The line got to forty-plus people before a few cars with room for two or three took one or two. The canary wagon got hung up on the parking lot apron and finally rattled up as the Elvis woman to my right commented she froze in it yesterday. The slug vet with his trainee to my left said, "Yeah, we didn't have heat all the way in!" In-Your-Face crossed with a friend and, as a result, steered clear of the line, intercepting the sidewalk past the No Parking sign near the mailbox. Spitter was quiet, in knit cap, coat collar turned up, the other side of the Elvis woman. I and the newbie got a civilian driver nursing a cup of coffee in a nicely warmed big Oldsmobile. I shared the accident I heard, a tractor trailer on the right side, northbound, I-95, after he got into the left lane, and the right lane was solid past Occoquan Road. He decided on the Lorton route, and it worked well. It was nice to drive through country before rejoining the maddening rush. There were remnants of a two-car collision and fire on one, southbound, I-95. Three police cars.

Going home. With only street shoes on and many areas of large puddles or soft/hard snow I had to pick my way from Crystal City to the slug line carefully. As I leaped the common nose-in parking dividers of piled snow (or stepped on it), I saw no Tackett's Mill line. As I rushed forward, I saw a lengthy Potomac Mills line—but no Tackett's Mill line. Then I saw some slugs I recognized taking the bus, who said to me, "The line is over here!" Actually, it was a guy from my office who had come in well after me. What was he doing over here already? The line was in front of the bus stop, displaced from the piled snow from the street plows. A bus or two pulled up right in our face and stayed a long time, blocking us from pickups, showing the bus driver's disdain for the whole slug process. Two or three women insisted on positioning for bus pickup, with no place marked. Finally got a sedan with another slug. Driver was gray-haired, with a close-cropped beard. He played classical music. He mentioned *they* really make it difficult to pick up, and I said, "Yeah, slugs are not recognized as a problem, like hunger and homelessness." I soon was immersed in reading *Lord of the Flies*.

Wednesday, 17 March 1993

Steady rain. Somehow I arrived in line fourth at 0520. Didn't intend to be early, just stumbled through the morning procedures of shaving, dressing, feeding the cats, and going. Spitter was first in line. All slugs bore their umbrellas. We stood on hard-packed snow. Older civilian slugs were on my left and right. The Elvis woman lined up next, then a young blond girl. The heavyset black woman with shawl crossed over. A minivan picked up three. I and the vet (without indoc guy) got in a four-wheel-drive Jeep after tilting the seat forward for him to get in back. The floor was uneven to accommodate the drive train of this vehicle. Very unsettling. The console sported a line of selections and a lit diagram of the drive train. Two, four, whatever combo of drive you wanted you could select. The driver was an Army lieutenant colonel eating a McDonald's-looking sandwich even though they weren't open. When he had pulled up, he made no gesture for riders, One? Two? Pentagon? Nothing. We've seen people go to the mailbox like this. It was very dark, with low clouds and steady rain all the way in. Christian Science Monitor analyzed several issues on the radio, including the Nut Hatcher getting endangered-species status to the aggravation of contractors and land developers. And news of the seven hikers in the Smokey Mountains who had been trapped. I thought someone should be held responsible for culpable negligence, for hiking during the snowstorm of the century.

Going home. The slug line displaced to the bus shelter again. The bus people were quite indignant, and one crabby woman became highly agitated that the slugs were not her bus line. She searched frantically for the end of the two-person line. The lead woman was probably the token taker (at the time, we didn't have SmarTrip cards to swipe, just tokens riders bought) as she was dressed shabbily and fumbled continuously with her source of pride, a bus radio reporting traffic conditions. I, the Elvis woman, and two others got into a new minivan driven by a smallish man with a big wife in shotgun. She was twice his size and sitting in the back; I couldn't hear them. Popular music played, but I wrapped myself in *Lord of the Flies*: Simon came down with the news the beast was a parachutist. But it was ill-timed, and he was killed.

One of the slugs in front of me was the short, chunky woman that had childlike long hair, only gray and scraggily. She almost made it three in the back row, but the man moved some personal belongings to keep us from being crammed. No words were spoken.

Thursday, 18 March 1993

Wind chill to negative eleven degrees. Very windy. I was fourteenth, after the Elvis woman. An Air Force captain, small guy with the cloth fore and aft cover (hat) and scarf wrapped around his face, with glasses, huddled to my left until I turned around to put the wind at my back. Oddly, almost everyone preferred to face the cold wind. Elvis woman turned also to back the wind. The steady rain the day before was all frozen, and the slug beach had dunes. Several cars took three, and after twenty minutes in the cold, it appeared the three of us would get the canary wagon, without heat! We all started cursing our luck when a small two-door Honda broke in the street ahead of the station wagon. A small woman with bushy dark hair allowed me in back and the Elvis woman up front. My knees had to stay to the sides as Elvis woman made no space concession. It wasn't warm in the car. I'm not sure it ever did warm, but at least the wind was stopped. A lone speaker in back played WLITE in a tinny way. Halfway in, she fussed around and brought out a phone, talked, but I couldn't hear for radio and car noise. It was light out, so I broke out *Lord of the Flies* and read about Jack's attack on Ralph to take Piggy's glasses. This book always reminded me of *Mutiny on the Bounty* when the mutineers were stuck on an island together and what they degenerated into. I inconvenienced Elvis woman to get out amid the driver's joking about having any legs left, after being cramped the whole trip, just as I did.

Going home. The slug line was almost back to normal. It had to conform to some piled rock-hard snow pack. I got in line behind the woman who had been with the ear-ringed high school guy. She was talking with a different young guy not in the slug line. What the —— is going on here? He left, and she turned to put her back to the easterly wind, and to the head of the line. I had my knit cap on and my lunch bag in my pocket, so I was relatively comfortable despite the wind chill factor. She made some comments about the cold and tried to huddle under her coat collar. She, I, and the Army officer behind me got in a huge, ole, white, well-worn Cadillac. A small wicker scent basket swung from the rearview mirror. The driver was a burly, older guy that played popular music. I rode shotgun, and the other two got in back. I finished *Lord of the Flies*, at least to the rescue, as we arrived at Tackett's Mill.

Friday, 19 March 1993

Eighth in line at 0520. Cold as yesterday but less wind. A mustached civilian was on my right, and spitter joined on the left. We spoke briefly about the line. Then talked incessantly with the purple-knit-capped guy to his left about Go-Kart and dirt bike racing. My fingers and toes were cold by the time a sedan of recent vintage pulled up and took three, with me last. I was in the back left, and it never did get warm enough to take away the cold feeling in my toes. The driver was somewhat erratic, being a younger man—about twenty-five to twenty-nine, I'd guess. He turned right from the left lane at the first light. Ran the left lane to Hechinger's and then cut in. Then after making the corner turn lane, jumped again. I wished I could whack him with a baseball bat! Jerk!

Monday, 22 March 1993

Cool, partly cloudy. Could see your breath, but it wasn't uncomfortable. A Navy chief was on my right; a coughing Air Force officer in his leather flight jacket on my left. I was early arriving at McDonald's. Eighth as I counted as I left my car. But people came from every direction, it seemed, and I ended up about fourteenth.

One guy literally ran. I thought I would have the last laugh as first the big blue truck with the retired computer geek, another car, and then Dorothy. I leaped out of line, but there were two guys and one black woman ahead. I got back in line, chagrined. I explained to the chief and SAC man she drops off at my door at work. SAC man asked how long the walk was from the off-ramp. Ten minutes. "Wow!" he said. I laughed at a two-door car pick up and commented to my slug mates, "I hate those two-door cars!"

Chief said, "Yah, they are a pain in the butt!" Pun intended, I wondered? Then the small two-door sports car pulled up. SAC man volunteered for the back, and I rode shotgun. It was the clean-shaven guy with glasses and casual clothes. He stayed left until Hechinger's and elided so smoothly I didn't notice when it happened. The irregular rectangular shape surrounded the headlight. I wanted to knock it off the hood. No words were spoken until the HOV segregated lane on ramp where a policeman was talking with a pulled-over motorist, twirlies going. The driver cracked his knuckles distinctly one at a time and scratched his crotch and drank coffee from a 7-Eleven mug. The radio played popular music and the news of Woody Allen and Mia Farrow custody fight. Also that he won best actor for *Husbands and Wives* in some awards ceremony. It was full daylight by the time I was dropped off. It was partly cloudy, obscuring the rising sun. I tried to get the make of the car but just got GTE and metallic blue as it drove off.

Going home. As I crossed Army-Navy Drive and the plethora of intersecting roads under the I-95 overpass near the Pentagon, another older civilian was taking my cue on darting across on the rear of the cars clearing ahead. After several of these sprints between the cars, he was near me and said, "Boy, I'm from DC, but the traffic's not like this. It's like they're trying to hit you!"

I said, "Yeah, the safest attitude to take is that each driver has you targeted."

We talked, and we hustled across in front of a bus on the south parking perimeter road and through the parked cars. He was going to the bus stop. As we approached, I saw no line and a minivan and car waiting. Wow! As I got near the van, I saw a woman in the front right motioning to hurry up. I jumped in the back of the Chevy van, I think, as it had captain chairs and seat belts that worked right to left. The driver was a Coast Guard officer. We all bantered momentarily about where was everyone, and isn't this great for slugs? Then the woman in shotgun slumped to sleep, and I took out the Bible to read Jeremiah. I looked up a few times and couldn't help noticing the woman's hair was very well done—light brown with curls and a bow. Jeremiah bemoaned the fact the Lord chose him to put out His Word. He cursed the day he was born and even the man that brought his father the news. The radio was on the oldies channel and a traffic report explained there was an accident at the Occoquan (River). Traffic was bumper-to-bumper crawl. The driver let us off on the wrong side of McDonald's, but we are slugs and no complaint was voiced.

Tuesday, 23 March 1993

I was tenth in line at 0520. Cloudy with promised rain not here. Not cold yet, but you could see your breath. Yesterday and today I noticed the slug line about forty people long before I left it. This is absurd. If I get in line at 0520 and get picked up at 0540, twenty minutes in line. I wondered about a 0600 departure. In-Your-Face crossed today, as yesterday, north of the slug line. Maybe he's reformed. There was no DCBCEC van or Dorothy this morning. A van, a couple of cars, and then I and the civilian in trench coat next to me got the Air Force captain driver with a tall major in shotgun. They talked continuously as before. I could not make out their words as the radio was in the rear speaker. The bespectacled, mustached, trench-coated guy to my right was soon breathing heavy in sleep. As we attained freeway velocity, I lost even the radio as car and road noise drowned out everything else. As I got out at the bottom of the off-ramp, I looked at the car make—a Honda. A compact one as my knees were up against the driver's seat, and we hit as we got in back. I was at work by 0605. Police in the Army-Navy lot parked head to tail for "donut talk."

Going home it was nasty out! Rainy, cold, and gray, dark overcast with fog. The line moved quickly, and I got Mr. and Mrs. Army in a very small car, Le Car, I think. A big heavyset white woman had to get out to move the seat forward and allow me to distribute my limbs and gym bag. The driver was a big Army guy, replete in Army cammies. And cloth cap, strictly and rigidly on his head. I groped and finally found the seat belt hopelessly tucked under the seat. The seat would have to be moved to get the belt out. They blamed each other for being two minutes late when we encountered all five (regular and HOV) lanes at all stop. I was well into Jeremiah by then and paid only passing interest to this aggravation. Mr. Army asked his wife for something to read while we waited, and she provided him an *Army Times* newspaper. After an indeterminable delay, the HOV lanes were released. Funny, I still arrived at my car at 1610. Awfully good for an accident. As we were released in the regular lanes, you could see about six cars all askew and dented. A multicar accident. Must have looked like that for the Iraqis during Desert Storm. The radio played popular music and reported another major accident on the outer loop. Then there was a fender bender with two stopped cars, northbound. At Tackett's Mill McDonald's advertised a blizzard and double cheeseburger, ninety-three cents.

Wednesday, 24 March 1993

Only a small island of snow left as I took sixth at 0517. I gotta get a better job. Spitter was number two. The first and second cars took three, and I found myself in a sedan, left rear. A civilian, coated, I think, with close-cut hair, was driving. An Air Force colonel was in shotgun and a tall Navy guy in long blue overcoat. Classical music, "Blue Danube," speaker on my left side. No words, I dozed fitfully until alarmed. We were on the off-ramp. My body recognizing the correct sequence of motion to wake up in time.

Going home, I was sixth on a spring-like afternoon. I got to third when I saw my neighbor coming toward the line from the Pentagon. I never expected to see her here and did a double-take.

She got in line about tenth, and I asked her if she needed a ride from McDonald's home, expecting to wait for her at Tackett's Mill. She suggested I move back in line, give up about six places so we could get the same car. I did, and we got a big car with an Army driver in cammies and a Confederate Civil War cap. A slight build, receding hairline guy in a trench coat with a black canvas bag got in front, shotgun. He was a slug vet going home, but I noticed him crossing the street to catch the bus in the morning. In tennis shoes. I think the bag held his office shoes, just the way many women exchange for heels at work. He had a mustache, too, so he looked a lot like me, big nose, and receding hairline being prominent features. My neighbor and I talked all the way home about the neighborhood and our kids.

Thursday, 25 March 1993

Cool, but nice out. The street light was out in front of McDonald's as I assumed number seven in line. Spitter was at the head and a SAC man (Air Force), on my right. He said, "Hi!" as I got close and proceeded to cough numerous times, just as he did in a car a couple days ago. That's what he gets for wearing that lousy leather Air Force issue jacket when it's really cold out! Better to look cool than be warm. I noticed the canary station wagon being parked. I guess he's a slug today. I was head of the line when Dorothy pulled up. And even though there were thirty people in line, no one volunteered for Crystal City. Then a Navy commander at the end came forward. Dorothy talked incessantly the entire trip so I didn't get to doze. She was playing classical music, explaining, "I don't like violins!" She was looking forward to her AWS (alternate work schedule) Friday off. And a big move to Mechanicsburg meeting for NAVSUP. She ascertained JP-1 for the commander drop-off point, and then we didn't hear from him the rest of the trip. Traffic was light. She mentioned she could retire in two years and wouldn't move. I asked her about Kevin F., and she said he had a Pentagon job now.

Going home, I walked over with colleague and his daughter. Army-Navy building was in evacuation mode for a bomb threat.

People across the street, dogs, etc. on site. They and I picked up by Volvo woman, middle-aged. Most of us commuters are. She worked in the Army-Navy building and said they found a satchel of explosives. She described going for gedunk despite a ban on elevators and to vacate. Volvo interior was butterscotch, and she complained it was a lousy car although it was paid for and turned one hundred thousand miles recently. We talked half the way home about cars, traffic, HOV.

Friday, 26 March 1993

Two Air Force colonels to my right (blue summer jackets and p'cutters—military slang for the cloth cover that can be tucked into your belt when not worn), black woman to my left. She stood off sidewalk to avoid my breath. Which you could see. IMF—International Monetary Fund—van came. There were three others finally, with thirty or so behind us. One colonel took rear seat, I shotgun, of Toyota Celica with irregular headlights. I asked driver in red windbreaker, and it was a '91 but looked like a 1993 (new). Cramped though. The colonel asked me to move my seat up. I did but felt otherwise. Driver said his wife wanted bells and whistles. DC 101 radio all the way in (a crass, loud rock station). Scratched his crotch, drank from a Seven-Eleven cup, and finally, near the Navy Annex (next to the Pentagon), cracked his knuckles loudly. Creatures of habit all. I was dropped off at the light at the bottom of the I-95 off-ramp, car behind honking in protest.

Monday, 29 March 1993

In line, fifteenth at 0520. Thought I was ahead of schedule as I didn't feed the cats this morning. A Buick LeSabre, big car, picked me and a civilian to my left up. The driver was familiar, either as a driver or slug. Middle-aged man in jeans and light sports jacket, he sipped from a mug continuously and fiddled with the radio. WMZQ country music: "A midnight girl in a sundown town . . ." droned a woman's voice. Popular music was playing a few minutes, then Gordon Graham, CNN news. David Koresh continued his stand-off, ATF arresting a guy trying to get in and defending the fact they didn't shoot their own guys or use military attack methods. The congressional hearings on gays in the military is bringing out all sorts of protesters, saying Clinton is changing his mind after seeing living conditions on the Roosevelt aircraft carrier. Chance of rain, overcast morning, in fifties. Besides sipping his drink and changing radio stations, the driver kept adjusting the temperature controls, but overall, it got very warm. I was still in my trench coat and wondered if I could hold out until we arrived. It was hot. He also lurched the car, trying to get into and out of lanes. As we passed the now-defunct Hechinger's on Old Bridge Road, I saw the cramped sports car guy's car. It had the plates SRR CPA. Five or six cars were lane jumping, slowing down those waiting patiently in line. I saw a Florida license plate as I got out at the bottom of the off ramp—probably a Navy pilot as we (they) all kept their tax-free Florida license while in the service.

Going home. The line was under the bus shelter because some slugs were without umbrellas, angering bus riders. Got shotgun in a small two-door car. Read Jeremiah and how the Lord brought his wrath on His people for not being obedient. Accident near the Occoquan off on the right pull-off. A person on a stretcher and two vehicles dented up with an ambulance.

Tuesday, 30 March 1993

Broken overcast, trying to rain. Rained off and on during the night. Fourteenth in line. A civilian mustached guy to my right, the shrimpy Air Force captain to my left with a briefcase and a big bag he could have crawled into. Again, about a twenty-minute wait. There were well over thirty people after me. Shrimpy and I got into a two-door Chrysler LeBaron, fairly new as shown by the digital mileage readout. An Army colonel was driving and seemed friendly, making a comment occasionally about the CNN news, which was broken and barely discernable from my seat, shotgun. Dropped off at the light.

Going home. About twelfth in line at 1530. These people must take the afternoon off to line up this early. It was a nice spring-like day, and I held my trench coat over my Bible and lunch bag. I and two other civilian guys, one very tall, were picked up by a newish Honda. I took shotgun and, after we started rolling, made the comment it must be a new car (drivers like to hear this). The driver, a smallish man with glasses, was in a dark, shiny (and therefore expensive) suit. He said the car was a year old and added it was his wife's; he usually drove a pickup. Classical music played agreeably. But he had air conditioning on, and it got colder and colder. Was this guy trying not to sweat? Protect his suit? Or what? I had my trench coat in my lap and finished Jeremiah, Lamentations, and started Ezekiel. I had no idea Ezekiel had the visions he did. It was like Revelations. A news break near Lorton caused him to comment, "That's nothing. I'm Air Force legislative liaison, and we took this group and that and even a mass delegation to a funeral. I have to admit I had a few drinks too!" Since the radio was weak and broken on my side, I could only assume the radio had made a comment on some unethical (typical of DC) practice like having alcoholic drinks during a function they shouldn't. We arrived at the Tackett's Mill McDonald's in good shape at 1610, plenty of time for a 1700 soccer practice for ten-year-old boys I was coaching.

Wednesday, 31 March 1993

Beautiful morning. Maybe a little cool. You could see your breath as I queued up about twelfth between two Air Force captains. The short one was on my left again. He had only a brief case today. I felt naked without my trench coat. A young girl in a black rain slicker reminded me I might get caught by rain this afternoon. We all observed a guy pull up in McDonald's lot near the pullout for the drive-through. He shut down the car and walked across to the end of the line as though to join it. We all thought like, "Hey, how can he do that? And why didn't we? Won't he get towed?" He came over toward me and the Air Force captain on my right and asked, "Is this the slug and commute line?" I explained this was slugs and the bus line was at the bus shelter across the street. He replied, "Oh!" and went back, got in his car, and drove off. He also was wearing a shiny (expensive) dark suit reminiscent of yesterday's driver. The IMV Aerostar minivan again kicked off the slug line pickup. Shortly, after a couple more cars, Dorothy pulled up. A big red-haired civilian at the head of the line stepped forward, as did I and the black girl who had three times caused me to miss Dorothy because she made the third rider to Crystal City called down the line, "Three?" I wanted to say "No!" but said "Yes!" instead. Dorothy was in a green blazer and only coughed once on the way in. She played popular music. Traffic news was of the inner belt of the freeway blocked off by a fuel tractor trailer shearing his wheels off on a Jersey barrier, rupturing his fuel tanks. Alternative routes were presented. The black girl jumped out at the stoplight. I didn't understand as I went as far north of Crystal City as seemed likely. I looked, and she wasn't heading for the Pentagon. A good scam, I thought, if it had been true. Jumping past twenty people to get to work.

Dorothy commented it was nice and bright out. I reminded her we would take care of that Sunday, moving clocks ahead an hour. She mentioned a carpooler from a suburb of Columbus, Ohio. I said, "Did he lose a bet?" I lived in a suburb of Cleveland when I was a kid and didn't know better. She lived in Cincinnati, and they were unfriendly, didn't give her a job.

Going home. Twelfth on a pleasant afternoon. I was comfortable without my trench coat. Mike, a regular slug, was ahead carrying on a conversation with a short man with a close-cropped mustache and red hair. Seems Mike wanted '91 baseball cards but the short man with a beach or golf umbrella held like a walking cane said he only had basketball cards. That Michael Jordan's rookie year card was worth $5,000 and that he and his son had over eight thousand cards in three years of collecting. An investment? A hobby? Both? Beats me. The short guy reminded me of a leprechaun. We got into a large car with all identifying marks of its make long since fallen off. It was blue inside and out, driven by a man slightly younger than me and had a large woman already in the shotgun position. I got the feeling I had ridden with them before. They talked the first ten minutes about their departure time and what route would work better. The leprechaun looked out the window while I dug into Ezekiel in the Bible. "A man like being of burnished bronze from the waist up and like fire from the waist down." I don't remember any music or radio. The driving couple were extremely kind, offering to drive the leprechaun down Colby, a side road closer to his house. He refused their offer as the rain, still ominous, hadn't started yet. Drivers of these acts of kindness didn't realize the benefit for one person was a penalty to the other slugs.

Thursday, 1 April 1993

Wow! Twenty minutes after getting out the door. In line, seventeenth by 0525. How I did the three miles to Tackett's Mill in five minutes, I don't know. I wore my trench coat as it was armed with rain gear. The weather was threatening again. A civilian in a very light-colored trench coat was on my right, the short black woman regular on my left. The black woman mentioned she liked it better when her husband drove. I watched a car take one. Then one take three, including spitter, without his knit cap. He was second or third yesterday too. Dorothy pulled up, and miraculously I managed to be the third. The same big guy with red hair got in shotgun from third or fourth in line, and a regular slug—retired captain, I think—got in right rear. Both dozed all the way in. Dorothy coughed a good deal all the way, popular music playing. I dozed on and off although it was light enough to read. She dropped me in the median in front of work at 0600.

A beautiful spring afternoon going home with a few distant thunderstorm cells. I arrived in line at 1530, but the line had already doubled around the trash receptacle. There was some confusion at the turn, and the line ill defined. It also interfered with the Potomac Mills line. The guy that looked like me (Glenn Curtis of aviation fame does too!) was ahead with his black bag, in tennis shoes, as was the submarine chief chewing gum and talking incessantly. His mouth moved like a fish's when not talking. And there were a whole bunch of people I had never seen before. Fair-weather slugs (FWS)! A FWS lined up behind me and Mike behind him. We three got a '91 Ford Taurus with an army, rank indistinguishable. He had Army trousers and a short-sleeved shirt with narrow insignia. I asked how he liked his car (because we had a new one at one time), and he was not down on it or encouraged with it. It was okay, he said.

Friday, 2 April 1993

Many slugs have Friday off. And drivers. It was drizzling, foggy, and cool. I queued up next to a familiar gray-haired Air Force colonel. Again, the young black woman lined up on my left. Like yesterday, her perfume, a spring-like scent, filled the air. One car per person until the IMF van pulled up and took three. Then Dorothy. I was about seventh now. The red-headed guy with long side burns was at the head of the line and took shotgun. I was in right rear; the black woman, left rear. We talked briefly about her carpooler who was late getting back from Columbus. Dorothy said this was her "early day." Off at 1500. The black woman said, "Me, too, at 1530. Wait, you work 0630 to 1600? Then I should be 1500 too! I'm telling my boss. They knew I stayed longer." I asked where she worked. NAVAIR? She said, "NAVOTSA." And Dorothy asked if she knew Betty Coxy in Code 10. She said she occasionally went there. We listened to WGAY all the way in. The black woman got out at the light for the Army-Navy building. I got out at the median at 0600. Red continued on with her.

Monday, 5 April 1993

Cold. Probably thirty-five degrees or so. Cloudy. As I walked to the line, I saw another slug also headed to the line. I increased my pace slightly and easily beat him to the eighth spot. I wondered if my cutting him off would make a difference or not. He was slightly smaller than me, in a black trench coat, causing me to look twice to see if rank was affixed to its shoulders. Someone in line had Colgate breath. You couldn't see it, but it was obvious someone towards the front of the line (upwind) had practiced oral hygiene. Spitter, with blue knit cap again, was head of the line. A civilian regular two ahead sniffled and coughed continuously. It was quiet a few minutes after I got in line, so much so we could have been standing in the woods somewhere. Imagine what that would be like; hiking through the woods when you happen on a slug line, standing patiently and quietly. Your position in line did make a difference today (I've seen one place difference result in a twenty-minute wait) as the gray-haired Air Force colonel to my right, and I got in the small four-door driven by the short blond-haired Air Force captain with major sidekick. Did this guy drive all the time? WMAL droned on the radio as the captain and major talked, but I couldn't discern. The colonel took the slug standby mode. Clinton and Yeltsin agreed to an aid package for Russia. I dozed and soon was dropped off at the bottom of the off-ramp to the Pentagon. In the office at 0610.

Going home. About tenth. Got to second (it was cold and overcast) when a minivan pulled up and took five. The older driver, an average to smaller man made some comment he ought to be paid for this. I said, "Check's in the mail!" It was dead quiet as the slugs belted themselves in. A slug has only one protection against a wild driver and accident, their seat belt. The driver then commented, "I've heard that before." The general feeling in the van, I think, was that I had approached that fine line a slug never crosses to offend the driver. There was no more talking all the way home. That argument that we slugs should pay comes up periodically. It would destroy this economic efficiency; besides, no one said he had to take five riders. As a matter of fact, the cars behind him may have been ticked off if they had to wait for the slugs to arrive.

Tuesday, 6 April 1993

Still uncomfortably cold in a full trench coat. Still overcast, but it didn't rain. I lined up next to the Air Force colonel again, this time the curly, gray-haired guy in black trench coat was on his right. A woman in gray to my left talked around the retired Navy captain until they swapped places. A couple of cars, the IMF van, and then I was head of the line with forty or so minions. A good line leader would immediately be picked up to expedite line movement, as if we had any control of what happened next. But as line leader, you felt responsible for stagnation. Several minutes later, a two-door sports car pulled up. I got in back, the retired captain in shotgun. I could hardly get in as my umbrella got stuck on entry. I immediately felt the seat on my legs and asked the retired captain to move up. He did slightly. The driver, a tall gray-haired man, must have been in his second childhood to be driving this car. Not slug friendly. When I sat up, my head touched the roof. Claustrophobic! The driver sat with his head cocked a little to fit under the sky roof well. He wore just long-sleeved shirt and glasses. News of an accident at the beltway and I-95 didn't sound good. No words were spoken until I asked to get off at the bottom of the off-ramp. The North Carolina Tar Heels had beaten Michigan, and Congress was recessed, holding up action on the president's stimulus package. I inconvenienced the captain as I got out, apologized, and left.

Going home, I was third in line. White two-door tiny car with Army driver and his wife. They talked continuously but undiscernibly while I read Ezekiel. Arrived at McDonald's in record time.

Wednesday, 7 April 1993

Full moon and one planet, beautiful night sky. Hardly any traffic en route to Tackett's Mill. Had the feeling you get when you're doing something entirely different from everyone else. Was today declared an off day? I was third in line, very nearly second after the gray-haired Air Force colonel with glasses, beaver-looking with mustache and bomber leather jacket. Part of that seasonal period of like schedules or routines, getting the same slugs and drivers. Same as the guy who swapped places to talk to the young girl evidently from his office. She came later, dishwater blond hair and some kind of heeled shoes that made a loud noise as she crossed the street and got in line after the Elvis woman in turquois or green trench coat. The first three of us in line got a large old car whose driver made no motion to indicate the number of slugs needed. I went around and took rear left, discovering a case of oil at my feet; I had to sit with my knees up uncomfortably. No matter, it's only a half-hour drive. Now where's the seat belt? There is none! The driver didn't wear his either. The captain did, and beaver didn't bother looking. The car looked older as I glanced around. The back of the rear seat was ripped along the top. The cloth covering the ceiling was stapled on blue with white dots. The light cover was off. The dash had taped cracks. It ran well, though. All identifying tags had long since fallen off, leaving holes where they had been. The rearview mirror looked dirty but new, with plastic covering both ends, like no one bothered to take it out of its bag or unwrap it. The driver had a coat with fur collars turned up. I never saw his face but did catch a part of his thick-framed brown glasses. His hair was parted oddly in the back. No words were spoken. No radio played, probably broken. Only the road and wind rushing by could be heard. Nearing the off ramp he made a talking noise to which the colonel grunted an answer. I asked for Crystal City, and he made more talking noises, and I somehow got the impression he had joked about slowing down and dropping me off while in motion. Weird, weird, weird! I got out at the light.

Going home. Walked over to the slug line with Hal, a colleague from our office, and his daughter, who works in the vicinity. It was a perfect spring day. Sunny and warm. We were third in line. They took a car rejected by a big guy with a circular fedora turned down. The driver had stuff in the front and a car seat in the back—drivers pull up for slugs routinely without any preparation for their riders. They crammed into the back next to the child car seat. The big guy and I then got a big car, but the black woman behind me refused to get in back. I was about to ask Steve, a former carpooler Navy CDR, when the big guy said there was stuff in the footwell. Wait a minute. This looks like . . . it is! The ceiling was blue with white dots stapled up. It was the oil in the footwell I had ridden to work with this morning! I was in shotgun, so I had a seat belt this time. It was hot in the car when we stopped for traffic. No air conditioning. Or radio. With bright daylight, I could look around and see different things. The driver was a fifties-looking guy with brown glasses. Again, he barely spoke, and when he did, it was indiscernible. I opened up Ezekiel in the Bible on top of the trench coat in my lap.

Thursday, 8 April 1993

One of our dogs was upstairs, and our son brought her to me as I tried to reach escape velocity. I looked briefly, couldn't find the leash, fed the cat, and left the house at 0520. Late! Traffic was getting heavy already—it increases exponentially, not linearly. I was one of four cars going into the McDonald's lot. Tenth in line. Signs at the McDonald's, bus shelter included one for "lost pair of glasses in a Celica last Thursday." Graphics were great. A tall (my height, six feet) blond woman to my right talked with the beaver guy (with glasses), and to their left, the retired captain and the shorter black woman talked. The full moon had a corona around it. The captain and I worked our way to one and two in line when Dorothy came and took both of us, with me getting in back. Dorothy coughed several times, and the radio played. I dozed. The astronauts launched last night, and Hillary's dad died. That was the news. Arrived at 0602.

Going home. Spring-like afternoon. Fourth in line. Dorothy pulled up. Two days in a row, the car I went in with I came home in too. Took Friday, 9 April off for camping and traffic avoidance of the Easter holiday.

Monday, 12 April 1993

At 0520, I was third in line after the curly-haired guy with mustache and dark trench coat and the reddish-blond-haired guy also with a mustache and glasses. The waning moon was bright in the morning sky, and there were several stars still visible. McDonald's looked nice, with huge Bradford pear trees in full blossom, symmetrically arranged either side of a square parking lot light. The black woman with hair in a small bob in the back and shorter than me by a foot. She and I talked briefly, or rather, she talked of her in-laws visiting and how she took Friday off. I told her I did, too, partly to avoid holiday traffic. She said she went to Belvoir Friday, and yes, it was very heavy. A car pulled up, but it was way too early (0530) to need HOV riders. The car had a driver and shotgun who asked for Crystal City. Three of the four people in line said, "Yes!" The reddish-blond guy and I were next and got in, me in the left rear. I couldn't make out the kind of car. It was four-door and roomy, a slug's dream. Both were Navy officers in blue suits, rank insignia undetermined. Amy Grant soon was on the radio, I thought, until every song was hers, and I realized these guys were different. The Holy Spirit led one to comment, after they had talked several minutes about cost, schedule and performance problems. I asked what program they worked on—E-2. I told them LAMPS MK III helicopter for me. And oh, by the way, I noticed you played Amy Grant, also a favorite of mine. I said people think she was a traitor, but I said I saw a talk show that pointed out she was leading many more to Christ by appearing to play to commercial demands. The driver asked if I was born again. After I said yes, the officer in shotgun said, "Praise God!" We talked of churches. Emmanuel Christian Fellowship? Me, the Vineyard Christian Fellowship. Yes, the driver had been there, and it was a little too dynamic for him. He had gone to Woodbridge Christian Fellowship. I said I had briefly, with the pastor for Joe Gibbs (Redskins coach). He said, "Barry Leventhal," and thought there was only 1 percent of the population saved. I said, "Yeah, the fear of appearing weird thing." They went to the cement factory to park for free so they let me off at the light nearby.

Going home. Caught up with Hal at the Pentagon lot. He swore at a guy bent on getting his car pool home. It was windy, overcast, and cool. Two cars waited as we reached the bus island. His daughter was in the first one. She rejected one woman as we crossed the street. Traffic forced her to go Springfield bypass and Lorton. Took us almost an hour. Hal provided directions. The radio played, and they talked incessantly as I finished Ezekiel, with the man of bronze showing him the excruciating detail of the Lord's temple.

Tuesday, 13 April 1993

Half-moon behind our backs in line. Partly cloudy. Still very dark. I was ninth in line at 0520. We seem to notice the weather more when one is standing around waiting in it. Spitter was at the head of the line. I was next to Curly and a short guy with a ridiculous goatee lined up on my left. Curly had a boxy briefcase, and Goat Man had a leather attaché. In-Your-Face crossed well clear as if reformed. The tennis-shoe guy that looked like me with his woman's shoe bag crossed, prissy-like. A short, heavyset, nicely suited man with a banded bag in each hand ran like crazy to catch the 0530 bus. The slugs watched in amusement. At 0538, Curly and I got an immaculate four-by-four. Squeaky clean. The Air Force lieutenant colonel driving held and sipped frequently from a mug in his left hand with WOWA on it. I couldn't tell if he was Air Force or Army in his short sleeve shirt, but his SAC jacket showed USAF on the name tag. He seemed to have a high energy level, switching radio channels when it got slow and driving fast and tight. His four-by-four was tightly wound too. He took the left lane to Hechinger's and cut in abruptly. No hand of thanks. I finally told him his car was either new or extremely clean. "Clean," he said, "it usually sits in the garage." I got out at the off-ramp at 0600, by the clock on the dash.

Going home. Weather was perfect. A nice spring day, ninth in line. I recognized only one other regular slug at 1530. The others were fair-weather slugs. Those who come out only when the weather is nice. I finally took left rear of a four-door Mercury Sable. Driver was a blond-haired guy in civilian clothes, no coat or tie. His wife, a heavyset woman, and he talked frequently. I read Jonah in the Bible and dozed, my trench coat in my lap, my brown lunch bag at my feet. An Oriental woman who had rejected a previous ride for reasons that weren't clear slept on the right.

Wednesday, 14 April 1993

Still cool. Running late, I leaped into line at 0525, ninth, next to an Army officer in a uniform trench coat. A SAC (term I use for Air Force officers) man lined up on my left. We all watched as the McDonald's employees opened up the store. Must be a 0530 opening time. A waning moon and a few stars could be seen overhead. After a ten-minute wait, Dorothy pulled up, and the usual three of us got in—the reddish blond guy up front, me left rear, and the short black woman on the right. Dorothy turned around to look and said, "You two are in the wrong seats!" She was referring to the fact we're usually reversed in our seating. Popular music played; Dorothy coughed and coughed. Not a fake one, but a deep one with phlegm movement. I did, too, occasionally. The car smelled of old Vicks and new cough drops. Neither from me. Swell, thirty minutes in a germ car. The radio soon reported the reason we came to a stop. A mulch truck had lost part of its load in the right lane. So why were the right three lanes whizzing past while the far left lane was at all stop? The DC shotgun man called police and told them he would strike again. The police traced the call and dusted the public phone.

Going home. Beautiful spring afternoon. Late leaving work. Two cars waiting at the line. A slug veteran black woman was in shotgun seat of a new four-door Honda. An Oriental-looking black woman was driving. The two black women felt comfortable with each other. It was obvious as they talked about buying newer cars (why couldn't I?) and some of their friends while a black radio station played soul music. With the windows closed and my jacket and coat in my lap it was hot. I began to wonder if the car had air conditioning. The driver opened her window. I'm not certain why, but it took almost an hour to reach the Tackett's Mill lot, normally half that time.

Thursday, 15 April 1993

Late! 0525 to the slug line, fourteenth. A tall Army major on my right, a short, young civilian guy on my left. He was casually (no suit) dressed in a jacket. We got a four-door car that the driver had the right front seat full of stuff. Don't these people prepare for slug riders at all? A car seat in the right rear forced me and the young guy to scrunch in the back. To which the young sandy-haired driver in gray sweatshirt apologized. We were behind the SSR CPA sports car (second-childhood guy), and the driver said this is the last time he was driving for a while as he was a CPA and would be working overtime. I thought, *That's strange. I would think the days prior to April 15—taxes due—would be the long days.* Anyway, he drove aggressively, staying left until Hechinger's, then jumping in and lane jumping to the on-ramp. The crowded conditions in the car (my arm was around the car seat, my lunch and Bible in the seat) lack of a seat belt, and now lane violations made me want to strangle him. I wondered what that would do for slugging in the area: "Slug strangles driver!" The young slug guy soon slumped and breathed heavy, indicating a good sleep. I dozed and looked out. I told the driver I needed off at the bottom of the off-ramp, and he replied, "I can't but can across the street." Sheez! Semantics. "Yah, that's fine." Damn bean counter! Must take everything literally. Another unwritten slug rule: agree with the driver as much as possible.

Going home. Accepted a ride with Master Chief Davidson, whom I knew from work; he was parked in the bowels of the Double Tree Hotel. We made several attempts to enter the building near the parking garage but were thwarted. Getting out of the garage was a maneuvering nightmare and reminded me of the "van incident" where I wrapped the full-sized car-pool van owned by one of our riders around a concrete building stanchion. I told him how to get to the slug line, and we picked up an Air Force officer while a van loaded fifty-plus in front of us. Or so the Air Force officer said. A big, fat woman got in first and constricted the loading of the other ten or twelve riders. We talked all the way home about traffic conditions, cars, and work. He had no radio. The Air Force officer was excited about his 189,000 miles, most from driving daily Lakeridge to Patuxent River. (The Naval Air Systems Command relocated from Crystal City near the Pentagon to Southern Maryland and built a Taj Mahal to work from on the already existing naval aviation testing station. Employees had to decide to leave the Navy/government or find a new home in Hicksville. It was a standing joke that all the businesses were owned by five or six family names.) Attrition through moving is a ploy the government uses to not offend anyone. It's difficult to fire or relocate government employees.

Friday, 16 April 1993

It was 0515. I just had my suit coat and plastic bag with orange juice and banana for breakfast and Bible. The veteran Air Force colonel, shining eagle evident and stony face on my right. The retired (I think) captain was on my left. The pear trees by McDonald's were still in full bloom. Overcast, humid morning with thunderstorms forecast. A young, slim blond woman crossed in front of the slugs. Then the prissy guy in a jacket. No sign of In-Your-Face. A car took two. Another three. Dorothy pulled up. I had been ninth. The reddish-blond-haired guy took front right, shotgun. The retired captain took right rear, and I took left rear. Dorothy related a very unusual occurrence: a pigeon dove to the center of her driveway and wouldn't move. Then there was silence in the car except for the radio playing piano classical music so low in volume I caught only a note now and then. We were all dumb-founded by the news of the pigeon dove.

Monday, 19 April 1993

About fifty degrees, without a trench coat, cold. It was that time of year where it was difficult to dress for both the morning and evening commute comfortably. Either you were cold in the morning or carried your coat in the afternoon. A civilian guy in blue jacket and light pants stood, his back to me after I coughed several times. I was just getting over my cold. A short young guy in a trench coat to my left. The black woman and then the shawl woman. The third vehicle was the van with captain seats and overhead strip lights. A little cushion and popsicle webbed with yarn, obviously a child's construction, hung from the rearview mirror. He took five, and I thanked him after sitting by the door, number five. He took the Occoquan-Lorton route very effectively. (There was a prison we passed in Lorton at the time; today is an arts center.) The radio was on weakly, so it couldn't be heard past the front seat. I got out at 0601.

Going home. Pleasant afternoon, eighth in line. Took shotgun in the four-by-four driven by the stout, heavyset guy in short-sleeved shirt and baseball cap without a baseball logo. This was the gear tight four-by-four. Two slugs got in back. I commented the David Koresh compound in Waco was attacked and tear gas thrown in to stimulate conversation. I said this going onto the I-95 on-ramp, and the conversation died before we cleared it. The driver chose not to play the radio. I had my lunch bag at my feet, my jacket over my lap. He had air conditioning but chose the window-down option. The back-seat slugs didn't seem to mind or took the slug mentality of not saying anything or complaining, just grateful for the free ride. I broke out my Bible to read Matthew again. It should be noted here that morning commutes were usually too dark to read, unlike the afternoon return route. I had decided to alternate reading the New with the Old Testament. The driver had one stubby arm out his window. His bulky midsection thrust forward. He was the perfect farmer as though he was driving a tractor. Never spoke. Stoic and stolid. We arrived in good time, and we thanked him as we got out in front of McDonald's by the twin blossoming pear trees.

Tuesday, 20 April 1993

A friend of the family was in town, and so I drove, leaving at 0500. I had to arrive early enough to reach the cement factory free parking area before 0530 at the northern end of Crystal City. As we arrived the long strip, usually occupied by cars bumper to bumper, was empty! Huge mounds of dirt occupied the area adjacent. Construction? I headed for the cul-de-sac. Wow, full! Many cars still occupied, their drivers waiting for their work start time. I pulled down a side street and parked ahead of a nondescript old van-like bread truck. The few free parking spaces were fast drying up even if you arrived extra early. Just shows what DC commuters will do to park for free.

Going home. I had to drive to the Bethesda Marriott to pick up our friend. It was a perfectly beautiful day. The George Washington Parkway was resplendent in spring glory. Picked up our friend at 1600 and returned before 1700—forty miles during rush hour! Only incident was a plank in the road on the beltway approaching the Springfield mixing bowl.

Wednesday, 21 April 1993

Cool, partly cloudy. Fourth in line at 0520. The reddish-brown-haired guy with mustache and glasses was first, curly-haired guy with mustache second, and the guy with a somewhat pointed nose (not big and bulbous, like mine!) and gray hair to my right. He stood very woodenly. Stolid. I coughed a couple times to clear the tickle in my throat, and he turned his back to me, his brief between his feet. Pinocchio was wearing a one-piece suit in a fine-checked pattern. Wind was from the south, left to right, me toward him. But it was very disconcerting him standing there with his back to me. Spitter, with trench coat, no hat lined up to my left and talked continuously to the Marine major to his left. Spitter, it turned out, has short gray hair and a very square jaw, much like Dick Tracey (cartoon character for you, millennials!) He had a large duffel gym bag at his feet. A large pickup truck in the McDonald's line kept headlights on us a long time waiting at the drive-through window. We all watched the young blond girl with ponytail open up the store. Spitter's breath smelled of, I finally determined, Lavoris mouthwash, wind coming left to right. A car took two; a pickup truck one. And Spitter and I got the car with SSR CPA license plate. The guy going through mid-life crisis. I took shotgun in the familiar sports car with rectangular headlights up, deployed. The casually dressed driver drank from a mug and played DC-101 hard rock. I dozed, and we were at the Pentagon by 0605.

Master Chief Davidson (work colleague) drove from Doubletree Hotel going home. It was misting, thunderstorms threatening. We picked up a foreign-looking woman at the slug line. I did softball and soccer scheduling and Bible reading (Matthew) until we came to a stop. I commented I should have brought my radio, believing MC Davidson's broken. He then turned it on, and we listened for reasons the traffic was stopped. Flipped pickup truck! Took one and a half hours to make the half-hour trip home. It was raining briefly by the time I jumped in my car at Tackett's Mill.

Thursday, 22 April 1993

Kinship (small church group) last night. Late getting to the line. Very cool out. About fourteenth, I lined up next to a tall Air Force officer. A woman with curly dark hair and a long bluish winter coat lined up next to me. (Even though she is behind me, remember, we face the street, making her *next* to me instead of *behind* me.) The young black woman and then the shawl woman. I felt tall next to the three women on my left, short next to the Air Force officer. The wind was strong and gusty, causing the women to back to the wind. I soon decided to lessen the wind chill likewise. We commented on the cold and wind. She then talked to the young black woman, who said we need the Crystal City driver. I said, "Yeah, where's Dorothy, the older woman?" I prayed for a Crystal City driver, and I got to eighth or so, and a car pulled up. Navy lieutenant commander driver who asked for Crystal City. The usually front-right-seat guy got in. I took right rear; the black woman left rear. I thanked him for asking for Crystal City even though it was more convenient for him to drive directly instead of having to stop at the Pentagon (or elsewhere) first.

He played an Amy Grant tape, and I recognized him as the born-again Christian. His gauges were instrumented like old voltmeters, long needles, finely incremented instruments. No heat. The seat was too close. I spread my legs to both sides of the seat in front of me. The tape was scratchy at first but got better. It was raining by the time I was dropped off at Crystal Gateway 3.

Going home. It was freezing. No trench coat. Temperature about forty-five, but the wind chill drove that below freezing. Snow had been reported in a few parts of the city earlier. Eighth in line. We backed to the wind, like horses, and an older woman two people behind me could be heard shivering, her teeth rattling! Finally, a new-looking Chevy pulled up. Astro took six of us. The driver, a tall, thin, young woman in a green-and-black-checked dress and jacket, wore glasses and had a lot of wavy brown hair. I took shotgun, and she seldom looked over, even when talking. It was wonderfully warmer in her van. My plastic bag with Bible and lunch retrograde and umbrella were at my feet. I made the mistake of asking her if the van was new, and she took that as a signal to talk continuously. I didn't. But she described the truck frame versus the Caravan *K* frame, the good deal she got (only eleven thousand miles!), and the only thing she lacked was an air bag. She was keen on her ABS after stopping quickly in the parking lot. Her fiancé and she had four girls between them, one six feet tall. She didn't like how big it was and how it drove like the truck it was. An intercom was needed for front to back comms; it was that far. Halfway home, she stopped for no apparent reason. None of the other slugs talked, two in the captain's chairs. She took the Occoquan exit, and traffic was light. We were all shy of traffic after yesterday.

Friday, 23 April 1993

Stupid! I heard the forecast for seventy-four degrees and so didn't take my trench coat. Typical spring weather has cold mornings and hot afternoons. Had to dress for both when you will be standing outside. Whereas a driver all the way in could wear a short-sleeved shirt, walk to the car and then the parking garage to the office.

Three cars maneuvered as I arrived in the McDonald's lot. Two for pickup, one parking rear end first. I zipped in, and as I got out, the rear parking car had the shawl lady getting out. I easily beat her to the line. I queued up 0525, fourteenth, to an Air Force SAC (Strategic Air Command) captain. I backed to the wind, which was gusty, and shawl lady did the same. The submarine chief bantered incessantly farther up the line. Cars in the drive-through caused the slug shadows to look like a human picket fence. There were few clouds, but the approaching twilight sun was enough to wipe out most stars from visibility. It was really cold. The line moved slowly, and I wasn't picked up for about twenty minutes. One of the slugging drawbacks was waiting time uncertainty. I got the guy that looked like my father-in-law, in a jacket, collar turned up. The old car with cracked dashboard, seats, no belts or radio. Or heater, I wondered. We were almost to the Navy Annex (next to the Pentagon) before I felt any semblance of heat. I dozed, arms crossed to conserve body heat. No one talked. I got dumped at the off-ramp light to the Pentagon.

Monday, 26 April 1993

Déjà vu! Fourteenth in line again at 0525. Nice morning with rain forecast. Young civilian guy in glasses on my right, an Air Force lieutenant colonel on my left. After fifteen minutes, another Air Force lieutenant colonel picked up three in a Volvo station wagon. He was eating and drinking his fast-food breakfast while MIX 106.3 played on the radio. News was of the gay march over the weekend and President Yeltsin's vote of confidence. I was dropped off at the light.

Going home, I waited for an office colleague, Master Chief (MC) Davidson. After ten minutes, I walked over with another colleague, Hal, and his daughter. I was tenth in line and inched up to fifth when MC Davidson came. He had office security duty, where you have to sign a slip on top of each safe to ensure it was locked. Then he was captured by a friend who officiated high school lacrosse and always had a story to tell. It was stormy, but there was a break in the thunderstorms as we walked over to the Pentagon slug line. Twice in the car on the way home, we ran into brief squalls while I read Matthew in the Bible.

Tuesday, 27 April 1993

Late, 0526, fourteenth in line. The short black woman to my right, the shawl woman to my left. We three discussed the cold forty-five degrees with a breeze for wind chill. The shorter woman had a coat and hood. She said she was going to be prepared today. I just had my warmest suit coat on. It was like holding your breath, putting up with the cold ten to fifteen minutes in the morning, knowing the afternoon would be more comfortable. I noticed the shawl woman had no shawl. During our conversation, she said, "I wanted to dress warmer today, but I forgot my shawl!" Right on, shawl woman! I told them someday I was going to sit in McDonald's and wait till cars are available. The short black woman said, "Yeah, we ought to take numbers going into McDonald's." We worked our way up until a woman offered to take three. A tall Air Force lieutenant colonel, however, used his hanging bag to keep the back to himself. Shawl woman said that wasn't nice, and I said maybe he'll be repaid with an accident. We all laughed, and shawl woman gave me a playful push. Luxury car, lights in the ashtray. Driver was in civilian jacket, with killer mustache. We talked politics and Bosnia.

Going home. MC Davidson walked to Doubletree. He picked up slugs coming to work, bragging he arrived at 0615. Ha! I arrive every day (well, most days) at 0610. He spilled his ice tea on one of the slugs on the way home. He always has a jug and a large cup with ice. Some kind of liquid dependency, I guess.

Wednesday, 28 April 1993

We are creatures of habit. I tried hard to get to the slug line at 0600 as everyone (other slugs) said cars are usually waiting. The concept was that at 0600 the slug riders ran out and the drivers exceeded supply, causing cars to wait for riders. I was up late doing state income tax. Instead, I arrived at 0545 and got in line about 0545 about fortieth! Sometimes it doesn't pay to experiment with the process. If it ain't broke, don't fix it! I was so disgusted I left the line and bought a big breakfast at McDonald's. With orange juice just $3. I was back in line at 0555, about twentieth. Cars came quickly as we waited in the forty-five degree, no wind cold. It looked and was forecast to be a perfect weather day. I finally got into a Dodge van with three other slugs—I'll bet the drivers behind us were angry about this not saving riders for them. The driver was a bespectacled, pin-suited man with a Naval Academy size and style ring on (they are very large and difficult to miss). I dozed and watched the scenery as it was much lighter out after 0600. After entering the segregated HOV at Springfield, the sun was yellow. The driver played several popular radio stations. At the on-ramp to I-95, a blue pickup was backward to traffic, police on the scene. I asked to be dropped at the off-ramp, and the driver, obviously not experienced, stopped instead at the end of the off-ramp, blocking traffic rather than pulling forward to clear the traffic behind us. Of course, this brought out a lot of honking from the put-out cars passing us. After walking over to Crystal City, I arrived at work at 0630. Still second in the office.

Going home. Early at 1500 to help with housework for a church potluck at our house. Walked with MC Davidson to Doubletree, then remembered my keys in my trench coat. We went HOV, and it was stopped frequently. Before HOV starts, many single drivers hop on, hoping to get farther down I-95 than they would if they stayed in regular traffic. At this point, because of this traffic shift, it's actually better to stay in the general traffic lanes, lightened by everyone hopping on HOV before it becomes restricted to HOV-3.

Thursday, 29 April 1993

It was 0527; I was twelfth in line. Starry, cool morning. The shorter black woman on my left, I lined up next to a man in white jacket and white trousers in topsiders. Glasses and tousled hair gave the impression he just stepped off a sailboat. I made a loud comment to the black woman, directed at him, about how there are a lot of new people in line and how we deserve seniority. I got to the head of the line—with all its responsibility to expedite the line—slowly. Easily, thirty people lined up behind me. Five of us got a Plymouth Voyager with options. I took shotgun. The driver, an Air Force sergeant, drank from a mug as we talked about our vans. He dropped us at the light, and I walked over to Crystal City with the black woman I was in line with. Just realized we slugs never tried to learn each other's names. Not certain why, but possibly it was a sign we didn't want to become personally involved in each other since we saw each other almost every day anyway.

Going home with Master Chief Davidson. I had to carry his ice tea thermos, a great big thing, as he carried his crock pot from a hottest chili lunch event, to the car. He really had an addiction to ice tea, somewhat peculiar. We picked up an Air Force officer at the slug line. Beautiful afternoon. We kept the windows down, and I read the Master Chief's *Tailhook 1991* magazine. I only got halfway through but enough to be done with the parts I was interested in. For some reason, we arrived at McDonald's at 1625, an extra half hour en route.

Friday, 30 April 1993

Cool, fifth in line. Crystal City guy with glasses and reddish hair, the solemn stone-faced retired captain, me, then the shorter black woman. I greeted Stone Face, and he felt compelled to grunt a response. I conversed at length with the short black woman until Dorothy pulled up and asked for Crystal City. The reddish-haired spectacled guy and I climbed in. The back seat and footwell had stuff in it, all of which the white-haired shotgun rider shoved into the footwell. Dorothy asked if we wanted to put it all in the trunk, and we didn't; slugs just want to go. The man with long white hair was in a suit, left leg folded over the right, cramping the slug in the seat behind him. I asked if he was the Ohio traveler Dorothy frequently spoke of, and he said, "Yes!"

Dorothy said, "They call you many things when you are gone."

And he said, "Good or bad?"

"Both," she replied.

He said, "You [Dorothy] are really trustworthy to leave your purse back there." We couldn't see it. Found it and passed it to the front. Police were at the Hechinger lot, twirly lights blazing. All the rubbernecking caused traffic to slow to the Occoquan turn onto I-95. No words were spoken, and I got out at 0605.

Going home. Master Chief Davidson took off early to pick up his wife. So I was back in the slug line, working my way up to the head of it, when a van pulled up and took five. It was the computer guy's van with the funny-shaped wheel wells. He had an overdrive button he pressed occasionally. I read Matthew from the Bible as he drove, windows down on this hot spring day. He said he liked fresh air—I suspected he was punishing us. Little did he realize the stoic nature of slugs. He didn't mention his work at all or turn on the radio.

Monday, 3 May 1993

Aimed for the 0600 window, arrived at Tackett's Mill at 0555, and the line was easily sixty people long! Cars were lined up six deep, though, and the line rarely stopped moving forward. All kinds were in line. Navy switched (this was the first day) to whites with short sleeves, but the other services as well changed—Air Force, Army, Coast Guard, etc. An Air Force guy with gym bag to my right, me with gym bag and soccer candy bars, then a young girl in shoulder-length blondish-brown straight hair and pink one-piece dress. The candy bars were to help fund our son's soccer team, just as other parents brought fundraisers to work for Girl Scouts, crew, lacrosse, swimming, etc. The young girl and I got a small four-door foreign car driven by a short guy with a pug nose. He ate candy rustled from his pocket continuously and occasionally drank from a plastic mug lodged on the dash. He jumped lanes from the left, then took Route 1 after seeing the tractor trailer–car accident on the Occoquan Bridge. You couldn't see the actual accident for all the police cars with twirlies going, but the lack of traffic beyond that area clearly showed a problem stopping traffic. At 0603, I was picked up, and at 0640, I got out at the light by the Pentagon. I had spoken briefly with the driver about the traffic, but mostly we listened to MIX 107.3. At 0745 the radio was still reporting all secondary roads (Lorton, Route 1) congested, even with the accident cleared to the side. At 0730, my wife took our daughter to school and couldn't even get out of our subdivision onto Old Bridge Road, the nearest major artery, as traffic had backed up over five miles from Tackett's Mill.

Going home, about tenth. We, the early slugs, could never understand why there were so few slugs at 0530 in the morning but there were always many more slugs going home at the same time as us. I was the only slug this afternoon, though, when a small two-door car with a loose hatchback arrived. It rattled violently but was of no concern for the driver, a thinish young man who was nervous about driving as he gripped the wheel with both hands. The shotgun passenger was of similar build. Music played, but the rattle and windows down drowned it out.

Tuesday, 4 May 1993

Picked up a friend who needed a slug ride with his car in the shop. Tenth in line, intermittent rain. He got a Volvo. I got a Rabbit, driven by a tightly wound young man with glasses. Drove like a banshee with 106.3 FM music. Started in the dark, but it was light out halfway to work. Talked briefly about yesterday's traffic jam.

Going home. Had a large Oldsmobile with a new used car sticker still on it. An Oriental woman got in on the right and spoke with the woman driver occasionally.

Wednesday, 5 May 1993

Tried the 0600 routine, trying to hit the transition from too many slugs to too many cars. About fortieth in line, but it moved so continuously we never came to a slug parade rest. Heels to the east edge of the sidewalk. A tinny sounding but newish Rabbit picked me up. A well-dressed, dark-suited man with glasses drove and probably his wife in the right seat. Scattered showers forecast. She had to get out to let me in. No talking all the way in as though some family secret might be leaked out. Radio played, and he stopped at Crystal Gateway North to drop me off and get out himself.

Going home half hour late because of work. At 1600 in line about twenty people long. I was at the end of the straight part, next to the Potomac Mills slug line. We all wondered if we would be picked up before the impending storm hit. It was dark to the west, where most of our weather comes from. The wind was from the north, yet aircraft were landing to the south at National Airport (this was before they renamed it Ronald Reagan International Airport). They were in stark contrast to the darkening sky behind them. I got into a car, shotgun position, while a bus was loading next to it. There was a constant battle between buses and slugs—we were taking away their clientele, although there were plenty of commuters to go around. In the District, there was constant friction, too, over surrounding county buses sharing DC streets with their buses. For example, the District would move an out-of-DC bus stop down the street to facilitate their own DC bus stops. Our driver was an Oriental woman who also sang along with the music on the radio. The slug guy in back slept. I read the Bible, Matthew and Mark. She noticed and asked what I was reading—one of a very few over the twenty-two years I was slugging. Most drivers either didn't notice or didn't care what you were doing as long as it didn't bother them.

Thursday, 6 May 1993

At 0525, fifteenth or so. Next to an Air Force officer and a short girl with heavily permed hairdo lined up to my left. Talked briefly with the officer—or rather he boasted of flying around thunderstorms and other great accomplishments—before a Buick LeSabre, white sports car, picked me up at 0538. Army colonel driver, lieutenant commander in shotgun. The car was new, and seats creaked of newness and new car smell. The dash had all the latest displays: temperatures, mileage readout, car door status diagram, and other bells and whistles. The back seat tapered like a classic contoured couch. Before we could go, a prissy-looking guy crossed the street in front of us and a young blonde girl in a long jacket-like coat walked woodenly from her car to the bus stop while we waited. She looked like she was on stilts or had no knees to bend.

Going home with Master Chief Davidson in the afternoon. We had to stop by the Pentagon pickup for a slug rider. The young blonde girl from the morning slug line got in. No radio, some air conditioning, some windows down; she thought we were brothers the way we kidded with each other. I didn't get much of Luke read from the Bible.

Friday, 7 May 1993

Twelfth at 0520. Smell of bacon from McDonald's. All restaurants precook bacon because it takes so long—I know that from working at a Perkin's Pancake House while in high school. Full moon with mostly clear skies. The ornamental pear trees in front of McDonald's were now with full leaves and no blossoms, obscured watching their employees. The black woman to my left and I talked about when the cars come and don't. Picked up at 0540. We got an LTD Crown Victoria—the kind police have. It was a big car with an Air Force lieutenant colonel and major. No words, no radio, no heat. As we walked to Crystal Gateway North (where I was working now), we—for slugs uncharacteristically— exchanged names. Hers was Joyce. In Your Face was in short sleeves. The prissy guy and the stilts woman crossed the street ahead of us, having caught an earlier ride.

Monday, 10 May 1993

Waning moon faintly visible in the clear morning dusk of a beautiful day. Arrived in line about 0600. Twenty-fifth or so. Line moved so quickly most marched Indian file, never facing the McDonald's parking lot. Got in with a Navy commander and civilian. Navy driver with balding rear spot. New Honda with white interior. (What were they thinking?) Played tape or disc of some famous male singer. When it ended, so did the sound in the car. The commander to my left worked assiduously at something. I dozed even with the daylight sufficient to read. After a long time, I looked up. Seemed like we should be there by now. You know the feeling, a certain amount of time passes, then your body recognizes where you usually should be. It was 0635, and we were by Glebe Road, in Arlington, about five miles to go. He was doing fifty-five? Unheard of. I had noticed his on-ramp manners: let everyone go ahead of us. Like he was driving an eggshell or at the risk of losing his driver's license for breaking a law. Arrived at work at 0645.

Going home at 1540, about fifteenth. The Dale City bus pulled up and spewed hot, noxious gases on an already hot, humid day. I'm certain the driver enjoyed that, part of the bus-slug dislike of each other. I held my suit jacket, Bible, and lunch bag and soccer candy money. I and two other slug women got into a boxy green Volvo driven by a short blonde woman with sunglasses. As we got in, she asked how we were, and we generally replied, "Better now that we were in an air-conditioned car on the way home." Usually, the reply was just, "Better now that we're on our way home!" The woman in the shotgun position and the short woman on my right soon went into slug repose. Like any good sailor, making best use of downtime. The driver kept looking in the rearview mirror at me as I read the Bible, Mark. I knew because periodically as she glanced back at traffic she braked or steered abruptly, as though just discovering a condition that required a control response. Arrived at McDonald's with no problems.

Tuesday, 11 May 1993

Tenth in line at 0520. Picked up about 0540. Stilts, In-Your-Face, and Prissy all crossed in front of us, well clear. Prissy had no suit coat, and In-Your-Face had short sleeves. Air Force colonel on the right, Army on the left. Van for five with light strips took five. Long wait for us. We got no seat belts or radio, with the old, cracked dashboard, and stapled on overhead cloth. Chubby driver was in the fifties throwback mode with a big ring on his chubby hand. I dozed the way in.

Going home. It was hot, sunny, humid. Buick LeSabre, butterscotch interior. Only two of us got in. Some slugs are too timid to ask the driver for three to help out so that the rest of the slug line suffers interminable waiting. Mobil oil cap and white uniform suggested the old gent driving was a gas station attendant. Oldies music, good air conditioning (yeah!). I read Mark from the Bible, slug in shotgun slept. Traffic stopped in general lanes before Springfield, and the driver responded professionally, taking byroads from the Springfield bypass. I glanced up occasionally but couldn't recognize the area. And then suddenly we were in the Occoquan-Lorton traffic line. It was 1620 but did well considering traffic.

Wednesday, 12 May 1993

0600 routine, parked out for a quick getaway on the return. Twentieth or so. I was picked up in five minutes and at the office by 0640. The sun, as I got out, was a foreign planet-like huge red ball at the top of the I-95 overpass.

Going home. It was hot and humid. Master Chief Davidson was at the Doubletree Hotel.

Thursday, 13 May 1993

Morning after a thundershower, cloudy skies. At 0557, I arrived fifth in line and was picked up by 0600. A small two-door Honda with a young black man with glasses and a mustache in a long-sleeved blue shirt. Woman to his right was wearing a peach-colored dress and glasses. Both were short as the front seats were drawn up, making the back seem large. At first, a black music station played but was soon turned off. The two obviously worked at the same place. He bragged his daughter made state finals—track, I inferred. They bashed a fellow worker who sounded incompetent, so they were setting him up to fail. After ten to fifteen minutes of berating him, they turned on a woman who was very opinionated (hers or nothing). They talked of publishing something, so I asked before I got out at the off-ramp; they worked at OSHA and produced a personnel newsletter. Important! I marveled at the scenarios played out in thousands of cars every day.

Friday, 14 May 1993

0600. Foggy, but nice morning. Newish Jeep driven by an Air Force officer. Have I mentioned yet the Air Force has more Pentagon employees than any other service? Not certain why that is, but they seem to place importance on dominating the Pentagon. Maybe to help secure funding, by being at the source. Well, close to the source. The Pentagon receives only what Congress funds them for. Water beaded on the hood, being well waxed. (Who does that anymore?) And a Plexiglas strip adorned it. He explained it had a bug divert function. I couldn't tell if it worked or not. WMZQ country music. "Marriage like a ball and chain but not to me." He drove herky-jerky, took Devil's Reach road and lane, jumped back and forth. Dropped one guy at the Pentagon for the subway and me at the light after coming back through the busy off-ramp. To park at a meter in front of the Army/Navy (paperclip) building! Thanks for nothing. Oh, we called it the paperclip building because each set of windows had a brick inset around them, making big, paperclip-like (long sides up) shapes.

Monday, 17 May 1993

0600. Nice weather, making our slug job of getting a ride less painful. Of course, there is a tipping or balancing point where fair-weather slugs come out, making the line extra long. And bad weather when there are few slugs, and you can get picked up quicker. Army officer (green pants with wide black stripe), rank unknown, as he was tall and slumped forward and left, keeping his shoulder boards out of sight, picked us up with his van. He conversed continuously with a guy in white sweater in the right seat. Van was not a Plymouth Voyager or an Astro. It had a built in glass recess. Music played, but I never did get the channel. Not popular, innominate. Driver's right arm did the steering, and he kept to the main route. Dropped at the Pentagon off-ramp light at 0630.

Going home. A small four-door white car. I took shotgun, and the short white woman, a slug veteran, took right rear. I had just turned down the guy who picks up his wife. It's an unspoken expectation that slug drivers will go point to point—in this case Pentagon to Tackett's Mill. But this guy would pick up a slug and make us wait for his wife to come out of the Pentagon so she wouldn't have to wait. One day, we waited almost half an hour as she was late. I added him to the "never again" list.

The driver, an Army sergeant, was a smaller version of my wife's mother. She slipped in the fact she was a longtime slug driver, a veteran of the routine, as though there was any value in that. A wild guy jumped ahead of all the slug line and got in, as though he knew the driver. He didn't. The wild guy was very loud and complained about not being treated like a Vietnam vet and about the air conditioning, and other amenities. She also took an Air Force officer to help the slugs in line. Soon the Air Force officer was talking with the driver, ignoring the wild guy. On a subsequent ride, she asked why we hadn't helped with keeping the wild guy out. We explained we thought he had a gun in his gym bag and didn't want to confront him without the police! "Swell," she said, "reminds me of the time I picked up a really poor man—not your typical well-dressed office-attired government worker. He really smelled bad, especially his feet." She kept her face out the window all the way in. We entered slug silence, WAVA on the radio, the religious channel playing. I read Luke from the Bible.

Tuesday, 18 May 1993

0557. No line? Thunderstorms threatening. A blue station wagon picked up an Air Force officer and I. Driver was a thin man with glasses and a mustache, in a blue shirt with thin yellow stripes, sleeves rolled up. A black woman in a red dress sat in front of me, in shotgun. No accidents, good travel time. Popular music played, scratchy and blurred. A slug never knows what level of discomfort they will have to endure for the commute.

Going home, short line. Brand-new Chevy of luxury vintage pulled up, with blue interior. Older woman driving and a man, older than me (at forty-six), in shotgun. He was eating a box of popcorn and kept looking at me. Eat popcorn and look. Eat and look. Unsettling. They joked about eating their lunch now, excuse them. He opened the center console and drank a soda. And kept looking. After I opened my Bible, he said, "What church are you from?"

"Woodbridge Vineyard," I replied.

"I'm from Bethany, and we just split. My son has an excellent worshipping voice, and I'm a deacon. Or was. So you have a good music program? I want my son in a good music program so he can exercise his voice."

I answered affirmatively, all the time remembering one sermon our pastor gave that was based on people looking for programs instead of a relationship with God.

Wednesday, 19 May 1993

Periodically, there are District of Columbia changes one cannot miss. The Indian at the top of the Capitol building has been taken down to refurbish. Quite unusual even though a replica is always available in the Capitol visitor center.

Car in the shop, so I wore tennis shoes, looking like a geek, to walk the three miles comfortably from our house to Tackett's Mill—0525 to 0610. Surprisingly, cars were waiting for slugs. Newish Honda with a young woman in shorts driving. Played classical music. Chuck Triska, a church friend, was already in the car. We talked about paintball and other trivia, including how he was very busy with his start-up framing company.

Coming home. Light drizzle, fifteenth at 1550. New red Jeep driven by a black man, a sergeant in the Army. A Navy lieutenant commander put his briefcase in his lap and read a newspaper. On my right was a black woman Army sergeant, also very young. Music started popular and went to black rap. When air conditioning wasn't on, I could make out a peculiar smell. Not certain where it came from, but a scented pine tree hung from the rearview mirror, as well as a rectangular paddle-like thing that must have had something on the front. On any given day, a slug might experience unusual and/or objectionable sights, sounds, or smells. Let off at Tackett's Mill McDonald's next to my wife, who was waiting due to the drizzling rain.

Thursday, 20 May 1993

It was 0600. A friend Scott Bethel and I in a Navy captain's (he was in summer whites, black jacket) new Honda. Scott took shotgun and talked cars, kids, Quantico versus Belvoir, drivers' bad conduct. Popular music in my rear speaker ear.

Friday, 21 May 1993

0550, twentieth or so, but never stopped in line. Army Lieutenant Colonel did not ask for three. Many drivers just pull up and wait for something to happen. Others pull up and ask for two and/or a specific destination—Pentagon, Crystal City, Navy Yard. State Department personnel seem to all take the bus, a direct run Tackett's Mill to DC. The State Department is in Northwest DC, so the bus goes through the whole of the District getting there. I got in next to an older white woman who immediately went to slug repose. An Air Force officer was in front right, a black Army woman in a dark jacket driving. Roomy car, make unknown. Popular music drowned out by road noise.

Going home. Twenty people in line on a beautiful day. A friend (Hal) and I took rear of a gray interior Honda. He dozed as did the one riding shotgun, an Air Force major. Driver was an Army officer, military short hair. Regular traffic stopped before Rockville I-495 exit. I had my gym bag and stuff I needed for flying out on business Monday.

23–31 May 1993

Slugged to work, shuttled to National Airport for business travel, followed by the Memorial Day holiday.

Tuesday, 1 June 1993

0600, nice weather after a storm associated with a warm front that moved through. Parked at the end of the McDonald's line as another civilian got out, a step ahead. No one in line, but several people arrived as we approached. We got hung up in traffic mid-street. I saw the first car turn indicator go on and went, to the civilian's consternation, ahead of him. Quickly a large car pulled up, I assumed for three. As I got closer, I saw stuff in the seat and retreated to my line position. "Couldn't take three," I explained, resuming first in line. Awkward getting back in! A Volkswagen camper van, like in the old hippy days—long since extinct, I thought—pulled up and took the two of us. It had kitchen items all along the left side, pop-up top, retracted. A partial bed was behind us, open area in front. An older Army officer (I couldn't see his rank insignia) drove and talked continuously with an Air Force major. In what seemed reverse order, the younger officer talked of a daughter with a history and English report due as well as GREs on Saturday. The Army officer spoke of a young child that fell asleep then woke up when a dog barked, went to sleep, then appeared crying because he couldn't dive during a swim test that day. Once on I-95, they stopped until approaching Glebe Road. The radio played popular music the whole way in.

Wednesday, 2 June 1993

At 0600, like lemmings to the cliff edge, we arrived in droves. By 0605, I got in shotgun as another civilian got in back. It was a burgundy Honda driven by a thin black woman in tight sweats and hair tightly wrapped to her head, ready to run or exercise. I intended to catch up on my sleep, but we started a discussion that lasted all the way in. Actually, the driver talked continuously, and I tossed out incentives to keep her going. She had a car phone—remember those?—that rang three times en route, her daughter and work. She was a sergeant in Army disbursing and supervising seven people under her. One guy was especially slow at filling out vouchers, and she had to take it from him to get it done quickly. People called her Sarge at work and Mom at home, three kids. Said she was only human and would bleed like anyone else. Played a "getting nowhere" tape and started it over when it ended.

Most of us that commuted to DC had security clearances, but it was unusual to talk about work because, as the Navy saying goes, "Loose lips sink ships!" And our security training said not to. So most of us avoided it.

Going home. A new gray Dodge Caravan, two thousand miles. Woman took two, then decided (after taking two women) to take me. Driver and I talked minivans for a while. We had a Plymouth Voyager, ironic since I told my wife I would never get a Dodge Caravan. Then I found out it was a marketing ploy to name the same model differently. The Dodge Caravan and Plymouth Voyager were the same vehicle! She was erratic with air conditioning, and it was alternately hot and cold all the way to Tackett's Mill.

Thursday, 3 June 1993

Crossed the parking lot and street in foot race with submarine chief that talked endlessly and always chewed gum. He in whites and black raincoat as a light drizzle fell. He barely beat me to about eighth in line, then a car asked for one to Crystal City, and he was gone. Could have been me. I got to about fourth when another car called for Crystal City. I got in a Toyota alone, two apparently in front. Shotgun acted goofy until sleeping. Driver chose left at Occoquan and Lorton. Worked well although Route 123 was solid and he didn't thank person who let him back in traffic. "Who was going to Crystal Park 3?" I didn't know where that was, so I got out near the Marriott Crystal Gateway and finished walking to the office.

Going home. Navy enlisted driving, young flirtatious woman in front right, Army fatigues on my right. We all discussed the advantages of HOV. Two cars had been pulled over by marked police cars. HOV was twenty minutes old.

Friday, 4 June 1993

0550. Partly cloudy, gym bag, umbrella, tenth or so. Picked up by Navy red-haired commander with enlisted Navy in whites. They asked for Crystal City. Toyota was roomy, the radio played, lost in road noise at speed. All conventional routes. Dropped at CG-3 boulevard divider. They were headed for Crystal Mall 3.

Monday, 7 June 1993

It was 0608, and I was running late. Gorgeous day. Forecast was eighty to eighty-five degrees. I took last McDonald's line spot right behind a BMW that took her time parking. Commander van driver with Air Force lieutenant colonel. Loose slugs grabbed cars at will. Line of cars leaving Tackett's, buses maneuvered around to get out. Driver illegally turned right, took left at Occoquan, Route 123 to Lorton. Vibration at door on my right, country music, no talking. Mustached driver had yellow-tinted glasses. Turned right and dropped me at the parking lot entrance one block west of the stoplights.

Going home. Start of line double-back. Saab 900 picked me and foreign-looking woman up. She was ahead as he pulled up left of the island. She picked back seat, which is what I wanted. Just to sleep and awake back at the parking lot. Like a time machine. Air conditioning was good, and he played music, but I hardly noticed as I read Washingtonians for getaways. Woman asked and got a Burger King drop (around the corner from McDonald's).

Tuesday, 8 June 1993

Off to drive for the Bellevue Housing Thrift Store, helping with repairs at the single mothers with children housing.

Wednesday, 9 June 1993

0600, very thick fog. The lemming routine. Many people were flocking to the slug line all at once. Moved quickly and got a black sports car with an Air Force sergeant driver with military short hair. Another civilian got in back. As might be expected for a sports car, it was very limited in room. Makes you wonder what people are thinking when they pick up slugs. Wrap around console. Played 107.3 rock music on the radio with news. Cleveland Indians won (from Cleveland, Ohio), Bulls versus Suns today. Occoquan, Lorton cut through.

Going home. Line was ten people long, slow moving and standing in Dale City bus exhaust with a hot sun. Retired captain behind me tapped my shoulder to indicate a ride was behind us. He got in first and jumped to front right, near the air conditioning. Someone I knew, Andy Fisher, was driving and said hi as I sat down, surprising me. Normally, slugs get in without looking around much. He then announced he was not spending $800 to repair his air conditioning on a $1,000 car. Temperature was over ninety degrees with humidity over 75 percent. It was a sweat box, awful. I closed my window to avoid a wind beating of nothing but hot air.

Thursday, 10 June 1993

Long line of cars at 0600! Air Force colonel driving big '91 Jeep Ranchero, which was like new. He played classic music, occasionally switching to news and other channels. When a slug gets a comfortable ride, it's like winning the lottery. Mainly because we get our share of tormented rides with something—or several things—wrong.

Going home. Master Chief Davidson provided the car—no radio, weak air conditioning. Hot outside, ten to fifteen people in the slug line. We picked up one rider.

Friday, 11 June 1993

Long line at 0600? Go figure! Overcast, temperature in the seventies. Nice morning. Short fat woman and a Navy captain waiting at the head of the line for Crystal City! Slug vet was a stout woman with straight, dark hair and a new very unattractive woman. Middle-aged civilian in a long-sleeved pinkish shirt picked us up. Male baldness pattern in the back. Honda, cream interior with a black dashboard. He played a Ray Charles disc to the end, then didn't play anything. Traffic slow for a southbound accident—rubbernecking in the I-95 northbound lanes. A semi-tractor trailer kept us from seeing much of the accident as we pulled near. Looking under was a large old car turned around with ambulance and police. Driver was a lane jumper and kept the car very cold. Outside air would have been okay, but you could hang meat in this guy's car.

It's a curious footnote to slugging that you had to dress for both the weather and whatever extremes the slug driver chose in temperature control. So it wasn't unusual for slugs to stand in line in short sleeves, holding a jacket or sweater.

Going home. It was 1535, hot, cumulus clouds build up. Two Army officers and I got the baseball capped, short-sleeved Jeep driver. Good air conditioning! Hot dog! Country music, darn! Traffic hosed up, long wait, and our driver did nothing, like take the bypass, to get moving. String of cars and police on the right side approaching Occoquan—they were all filling out forms.

Wednesday, 16 June 1993

Going home. Twenty people ahead of me. Finally, got a Pontiac Sunbird. The driver was very young woman in shorts. She apologized for the car being dirty. I was in shotgun and civilian in back. We discussed sun side of the car versus up front. Said she was moving after seven years, longest in one place, to get her ex off her back. Her father was to buy house in a Woodbridge development, but it fell through. We took the Lorton cutoff from Springfield, traffic being heavy.

Thursday, 17 June 1993

Pleasant short-sleeved-shirt kind of morning. Last spot in the parking lot. Long line moved quickly. An Army captain took an Air Force officer in back, me in shotgun. Bench seat couldn't move up. Popular music, news, no talking. News included syringes in Pepsi cans, Clinton news conference tonight. Bulls won game 4, lead 3–1. Big car for a young guy. Oldsmobile, I think.

Going home, Bud Piland from our church home group driving! Some people you just never expect to see in the slugging process. Bud worked in Rosslyn, Virginia, so I never saw him commuting. I read 2 Corinthians, stopping to talk occasionally. He was going to Tackett's Mill to refinance his house. Accident near Occoquan, small car rear bashed in. Two cars and one emergency vehicle off the shoulder to the left backed up all lanes. Bud stayed left, and we eventually got through.

Friday, 18 June 1993

Small line, then more cars than riders. Got into a two-door Jeep with two Army majors. Good air conditioning, WTOP radio. Seat belt didn't work, though.

After arriving back home in the afternoon, the flyer with a picture of a Volkswagen bug and a family of three with their dog in the car said the following:

> Attention Commuters!
> The ownership of Tackett's Mill Shopping Center voluntarily set aside 161 spaces for commuter parking. Over the last year, more commuters than the number of allocated spaces are parking at the center.
> In order to preserve the privilege of continuing to utilize this location, we ask commuters to use other commuter lot locations once the

161 parking spaces have been filled. The 161 spaces are located on Harbor Drive between McDonald's and the Tackett's Mill Stone sign. They are striped in YELLOW.

Listed below are additional Park and Ride lots: [Listed.]

*Designated parking sites served by the commuter bus.

Thanks for your support.

Potomac and Rappahannock Transportation Commission 490-4422

Monday, 21 June 1993

Cloudy, warm morning. Thunderstorms forecast. Twentieth or so at 0550. Navy supply corps lieutenant, Army lieutenant colonel, and I got in an ultra-plush Cadillac, silver with black top. Mata Hari, a mean-looking Oriental woman, was driving. 99.5 played on the radio, environmental controls activated. She controlled everything from her command center in the driver's seat. All the windows soon went electrically to full up. She obviously had a button for that. She touched pressure-sensitive controls to affect the temperature control. The seats were plush black leather. I had my Bible and red Coke lunch bag. lieutenant colonel was to my left; lieutenant in front, shotgun. She lane-jumped big time. Going to Hechinger's down Old Bridge Road and to the on-ramp, all the way cutting in repeatedly. Wish I could have arrested her. As I got out, I noted the license plate: JADE 9.

Going home. Master Chief Davidson and I walked to the Doubletree Hotel, where he parked. Explained he had a tough day listening to Craig (a GS-13 government employee from the NAVAIR Training Office, PMA 215) talk about softball. They split, but Craig was a hero again, holding them to three runs after a fifteen run lead. On arriving at his car, the master chief threw all sorts of debris into the back of his car, including two empty Dunkin' Donuts bags. Then he fussed with the ice tea again. You'll remember he took his "tanker" of ice tea everywhere as though he was afraid of ever running out and perishing. I asked him if he drank a lot of ice tea on ship, and he said, "Yes, the general quarters were difficult, and I had to use waste baskets to relieve myself!" Gross! I read Jude from the Bible and dozed. the master chief tried to start a conversation with our Air Force slug, but it was all in vain. He didn't want to talk, and the conversation died.

Tuesday, 22 June 1993

0600, partly cloudy, nice morning. I took second to last parking-lot spot. About twentieth in line, but it moved quickly. Just missed Commander Cable from our office and part of a car pool we had for a while. Saw the JADE 9 Cadillac, a very nice ride. Finally, I got into a Honda with burgundy interior. Older civilian guy with his wife in a purple dress and funky glasses with a dip in the stem to the ears. They talked about a formal exercise, placing flags, arranging food, etc. Cold, cold, cold in their car. Dozed, popular music on the radio, arrived at 0630.

Wednesday, 23 June 1993

Long slug line at 0600. lieutenant commander in the Air Force at the head of the line but not actively pursuing a car. Now seven cars in line, and he was waiting for one to pull up to his feet. There was commotion down the car line from a van. It was a friend, Hal, and his daughter in a Dodge Caravan, automatic, V-6, with options. Good air conditioning. Read and listened to the radio.

Monday, 28 June 1993

It was 0600, nice morning, thirty slugs in line. Moved fast and picked up by an Army major driving a cheap rundown Honda. Small, light car, flimsy impression. Black Navy commander got in back right; Air Force officer was in rear left. Played WASH FM, 97.1. Sun in our eyes all the way in. Unceremoniously dropped at the parking lot—thanks for nothing!

Tuesday, 29 June 1993

Warm morning, promising greater heat, humidity, and discomfort. At 0555, line was almost to the corner, sixty or more people, largest slug line I've ever gotten into. Moved quickly and was picked up by a Navy commander driver driving a Chevy Caprice Classic. A short young girl with glasses also got in. It appeared the driver's wife, in a flowery dress and very curly hair, was already in the car. We all dozed with a couple of sudden jerks going in. Popular music disappeared with the road noise at speed. I asked to be dropped off at the light at the bottom of the Pentagon off-ramp, but the driver said he had police behind him, so he dropped me off in the parking lot.

Tuesday, 6 July 1993

The news before leaving for work was of Mississippi floods, the president in Japan for a summit, and the Orioles lost 7–1. It was hot. Heat index forecast was 110 degrees. Uncomfortably warm at 0600 in line. Two-door car—a slug inconvenience—with an Air Force major driver and Air Force major in shotgun seat. I'm guessing this saying came from stagecoach protection. I didn't bother to explain the need to get out first. Oldies music on FM 100.3. No words spoken. Traffic was good. People still on vacation? With kids out of school, less traffic also from all their travel—students, teachers, and parents.

Coming home. Reached forecast heat index, so I left my suit jacket at work. Long-sleeved shirt, though, to guard against the "ice box" slug rides. Sweating while standing in line. The Dale City bus pulled up belching heat and exhaust fumes into the line. Why isn't the exhaust pipe aimed away from the passenger loading side? Blue 1980s Oldsmobile with excellent air conditioning. Popular music played.

Wednesday, 7 July 1993

Showers last night. Hot weather forecast continuously to the weekend. Welcome to DC in the summer. 0555. Long slug line, but it moved fast. Guy in shorts next to me, with short hair. Many slum to work and change there; it's a popular routine for Pentagon personnel too. Finally, got an Air Force sergeant (Navy chief equivalent) driving a Ford Aerostar. Excellent air conditioning! WMRQ music—do all chiefs like country music? Sun was a red-orange ball directly ahead as we traversed the Occoquan bridge repair work. Radio became lost in road noise as we crested the bridge hill. Chief drank from a plastic ship mug with flared bottom for added stability. The dashboard had a carpet cover—for sun protection, I guess. Older short woman in shotgun. Air Force lieutenant colonel to my left immediately assumed the slug transition phase or sailor marinization state of sleep. Soon after the radio reception started to fade, Chief increased the volume of the fluctuating country music. Powerball lottery $100M prize over twenty years with 50 million tickets sold in fourteen states. Chance of winning one in 55 million. Hockey tickets are increasing $7 each for season tickets and $3 per game. The Capital Center is now the US Air Pavilion.

Dropped me off after a right turn at the stop light. Said he was afraid to drop me at the bottom of the hill because a bus almost hit a car doing that.

Going home. Sweating in line. Bottoms of my shoes were hot! Easily 110 degrees. After fifteen minutes of waiting, the guy who waits for his wife pulled up. Hal and I declined his ride. We saw him waiting for his wife as we pulled out of the Pentagon parking lot. A short-haired Marine in civilian clothes—purple and blue shorts—played non-directional music and rambled on. Air conditioning was excellent, but sweat was still rolling down my back. Guy in shotgun with tattoos had his seat back too far, but I didn't complain—part of the slug credo. Just glad to have a ride. Interior was a light brown, not quite butterscotch color. Music was vibrating-my-chest loud.

Thursday, 8 July 1993

Snappy blue car waiting. Woman had just asked for riders and was rolling up the window when they said it was for Crystal City. I leaped forward and knocked on the window as she drove off. I got back in line, officer to the right, shorter, thinner woman to the left. Heat index was 100 degrees; forecast was 120 degrees. We got an Army lieutenant colonel in a Lexus, good air conditioning. Team sports radio played. It was stupid. Talking about the millions players get: one guy getting $18M over six years. That's $3M a year! Driver was skittish on the drop-off at the stop light, letting me off in the traffic lane. He had driven cautiously and conservatively. Unusual.

Going home. Oldsmobile with twenty-two-month-old mulatto child in a car seat behind the shotgun position. A white woman, she complained about her air conditioning, and we discussed kids and God all the way home.

Tuesday, 13 July 1993

Going home with the master chief. His car quit in the HOV lanes. Just stopped, and he coasted to the shoulder lane. A car stopped and offered us, his slugs, a ride to Tackett's Mill. He stayed to see his car towed away.

Wednesday, 14 July 1993

Walked to Tackett's Mill, slowly to keep from sweating; it was seventy-five degrees or so with humidity making it even warmer. In the brightening morning sky, Mars kept company with a crescent moon. I bought a bagel knot at the Giant Supermarket in the Tackett's Mill shopping center and got in line. Crystal City was asked for by a black woman driver with Oriental eyes and a Japanese passenger. The English-speaking woman I had seen previously in the slug line got in too. The black woman spoke rapidly, like the guy in the TV commercials. She directed her tirade at the Japanese guy, looking at him continuously while he looked straight ahead, like a nagged husband. Awkward and embarrassing for outsiders! She complained that her college friend of nineteen years had sent her a nine-year-old son and fourteen-year-old daughter to stay with her son and babysit a five-year-old. The nine-year-old son stayed up all night, crying; he wanted his mother, who was once divorced, and he wasn't used to a man being with his mother. She was twice divorced, and she closed the door to "get her son used to it being closed" when she had a boyfriend over. The daughter was washing two items at a time, and she explained she wouldn't allow that. It was wasteful. This went on for fifteen minutes with her expanding her audience by turning to look at us in back or looking in the rearview mirror and asking us if we didn't agree with her handling of laundry and the kids. No wonder we slugs preferred total silence to these kinds of family conundrums.

Thursday, 15 July 1993

Arrived at 0605 after walking the three miles to Tackett's Mill. Below flyer passed out as I got in line. Hot, sweaty line thirty people long. Japanese-descent driver in a Honda. An Air Force captain. Woman took shotgun, an Air Force Major to my left. No talking. Just the Oriental eyes in the rearview mirror. Xtra 104 oldies on the radio. Shuttle launch Saturday, with the president in Hawaii. Gays being allowed in the military decision Friday. The flyer read:

WHY COMMUTE TO DC EVERY DAY
When one or more days a week you could telecommute to your DC office?
"TELECOMMUTING" is the new energy-conscious, time-efficient way to *electronically* commute to your DC office without ever leaving Lakeridge.
WORKSPACES ARE AVAILABLE TODAY.

followed by a couple of paragraphs on where the Lakeridge offices are and who to contact. What they didn't mention is the follow-on question of why wouldn't you just telecommute from home and avoid this expense altogether?

Friday, 16 July 1993

Our car is back after being worked on. Beautiful morning, few slugs—it's Friday, and many government employees have off for an assortment of reasons: compressed work schedule (they work enough in the first four days they get Friday off), telework from home (if authorized and trusted by your manager), and because they work at an off-site location (supposedly). Two Air Force lieutenant colonels picked me up. Driver was new to the area, but his buddy was all-knowing about everything. I was embarrassed to be privy to their discussions. They talked continuously, slowly, with breaks. No radio. Talk was of preparing briefs and working weekends. One said he was working thirteen hours a day, and now the office was going to a ten-hour workday for a four-day workweek, which he would readily accept. One worked weekends occasionally, when briefs weren't done or approved in advance. The right seat, shotgun, officer explained my request for dropping me off at the light at the bottom of the off-ramp.

Monday, 19 July 1993

Long line at 0600. I was at the halfway point in a slug line that went around the corner to across from the Burger King. A short woman was our driver. Worked at NAVSEA and was traveling today. She took an Army officer to the Pentagon, vice walking from the bottom of the off-ramp as Crystal City riders are expected to do.

Going home. The typical unknown phenomenon: while many employees came in 0800 or 0900, they still managed to go home the same time as those of us that commute at 0600. Very long line on a very hot and humid day. You could feel the heat from the sidewalk through your shoes. Fair-weather (not raining or freezing) slugs were likely the reason for the long line.

Tuesday, 20 July 1993

Long line at 0600. Gym bag with lunch, got in a tiny, economy station wagon with a Navy officer driving and his wife, evidently, in the right seat. Very cold, condensation so thick all windows were difficult to see out. Woman had high close-cropped haircut and long military green dress. She sat stiff and prim and didn't look at her husband when she spoke. He started radio soon after leaving Tackett's Mill, and she cut the air conditioning off.

High heat index going home: ninety-plus degrees and over 80 percent humidity. The master chief invited Hal, Stephanie, and I to ride with him. We discussed a certain objectionable, weird government employee in the office.

Wednesday, 21 July 1993

Short slug line, moved quickly. Navy commander in a Honda asked for Crystal City. A Navy commander at the head of the line selected back, which was awkward as I came from twenty to twenty-five people down the line, most waiting for Pentagon. As I got in front the short, mustached commander with glasses gruffly stated, "You can move up your seat!" Not *would you, could you please*, or *if it's okay*, but "You can move it up!" he demanded. Driver had a yellow hand towel over his left shoulder. I didn't ask. Radio was on 107.3 FM, Jack Diamond in the Morning Show. And the air conditioning blew cool air continuously. Driver took the Occoquan cut-off, driving jerky and hurriedly.

Thursday, 22 July 1993

Going in seventy degrees, low humidity, nice weather. Woman to my right in slug line had fragrant perfume, was doing her nails, and had short blond hair braided and folded on her head. Here's someone who spends a lot of time trying to look her best, I thought. Many slugs read books or papers in line. Easy commute, dropped off at the light at the bottom of the off ramp.

Monday, 26 July 1993

Picked up an old friend from San Diego, Terry Cush, to drive to the Tackett's Mill slug line. Talked all the way in. Young black civilian driver in a Mercury Sable-like Honda. New and very nice, a treat for slugs. We, Terry and I, talked about not buying new cars while in one. Cloudy, smattering of rain on the ride in.

Tuesday, 27 July 1993

Took a day off to take the family to Delaware State Park Beach on a non-busy day.

Wednesday, 28 July 1993

Line halfway to Burger King again. JoAnn, an Oriental woman with black bouffant (brushed out, short) hair, a mustard-colored jacket and black dress, with colleague Vince (in short-sleeved shirt, tie, and glasses) in back left. A civilian guy got in back right, and I took shotgun. A Buick Grand something or other. Digital, recessed dashboard instruments, push button control panel. Both were EPA employees. She just completed DOPO, a contract management school. They both conversed with me the entire trip about how important the EPA was, how they were small with nineteen thousand contractors for support. They even have EPA badges and gun-carrying enforcers.

Thursday, 29 July 1993

Navy lieutenant commander, chunky, bulging whites, with Steve in right seat. They talked towed arrays (ship acoustic detection devices) all the way in. Air Force major in the back left seat. No air conditioning. I studied insurance all the way in. Inner loop I-495 beltway shutdown due to an overturned tractor trailer, but it didn't affect us northbound on I-95. I've noticed a decided decline in service personnel being fit. For a while, the Navy required a picture with annual fitness reports so that anyone not fit and trim could be considered less qualified in the organization ranking for promotion. Guess that's gone by the wayside now.

Going home. A long, long wait. Near one hundred degrees, high humidity. I could feel the sidewalk heat through my shoes. No wonder the early government took summers away from the District for its oppressive heat index. In line at 1530, picked up at 1600. Of all days to take so long. By this time, the line had more than doubled. Red sports car with rock music picked us up. Driver started a conversation with the young civilian, dressed casually for school. Said he drove dirt car racing for fun. I guess so as he drove very jerky.

Friday, 30 July 1993

Ten or so people in line at 0600. I and a heavyset woman got into a Dodge Caravan that could have taken two more. Some drivers consider taking extra slugs added cost as increased car weight takes more gas. The driver was an Air Force major, older-looking with glasses, and his wife was nicely dressed but stiff, stiff, rigidly stiff. No words at all, oldies music.

Going home, Air Force sergeant in a gray Ford Tempo. Radio said a bus hit a woman, and we saw a pickup hit a car in the regular lanes, which our driver stopped to volunteer information! Not in our lane, we just wanted to go home. We took the Springfield bypass, and he asked me where to go afterwards as I-95 backed up.

Monday, 2 August 1993

Blue Dodge Caravan, two clones in front—civilians with glasses and mustaches. Driver wore a short-sleeved shirt while the other guy had a suit coat on. Talked in low tones as though not desiring us to hear their business. Did hear "prepare the brief" and "get my work done." Like that was anything worthy of concealment. Radio was barely audible at low speed and completely washed out by road noise at freeway speed. No other discussions.

On the way home, walking to the slug line at the Pentagon a broken water pipe at the Route 1 overpass had six inches of water flooding the intersection, making it difficult to cross dry. On arrival at the Tackett's Mill, slug line sign noticed no one in line. Meanwhile, the Potomac Mills slug line sign was the length of the bus stop down the way. An Oriental woman driving a Plymouth Voyager picked me up so we had to wait for another slug to arrive. Another car waited behind us. Supply and demand!

Tuesday, 3 August 1993

In line at the second No Parking sign at 0600. Voyager with a smoking, thin woman driver. Slugs usually declined riding with smokers so that a smoker had to have their drag before arriving at the slug line. Little did they realize that nonsmokers can detect minute amounts of cigarette smoke. But at least they put them out before we get in. She had asked for Crystal City so that we didn't get an immediate response. Presently, two Navy officers, one a captain, jumped in. She was in blue jeans and dressed poorly. Said she was catching a flight and had kids. I told her the Devil's Reach alternate route should be used as traffic was backed up on I-95. She turned the radio on but played country music as opposed to obtaining the traffic report. When she turned the air conditioning on, we rolled up our windows, nothing said.

Wednesday, 4 August 1993

Left later than usual due to being up late. At 0610, I parked at the Burger King, walked through a wheat field of weeds in a vacant lot. Twenty people in line! I got a four-wheel-drive vehicle with a white male driver in long sleeves and a tie. Right arm didn't move, and he kept it in his lap, causing us to suspect he lacked full function. Three gauges on the dashboard: oil pressure, attitude indicator (like in an aircraft), and battery-charging indicator. Tight transmission. WMZQ, country music. We observed the Occoquan Bridge and roadwork and discussed their progress briefly.

On the way home, we were picked up by a short middle-aged woman in pink hospital scrubs. She worked at Columbia Hospital and had been up since 0300. Oldsmobile station wagon. Accident on the bridge between a truck and a van caused us to be late, 1700, arriving at Tackett's Mill. Hour and a half for a normal half-hour ride. I read the paper all the way.

Thursday, 5 August 1993

In line past second No Parking sign again, at 0557! Moved quickly, and we jumped in a car for Crystal City but unfortunately—after pulling away—found one slug was a Pentagon civilian. Just blew our direct drive advantage. Nothing worse than revealing a surprise after being in traffic on the way. The windshield had a crack the length of the windshield bottom. WMZQ country music. Probably just me, but it seems country music has dumb words to many of their songs: "Here's a quarter, call someone who cares," "When you go take your memory with you."

Friday, 6 August 1993

Cold in the morning! Expected no line but was twentieth on arrival. Like lemmings, several of us migrated to the line simultaneously. I beat a couple people when I challenged the oncoming headlights, not waiting for the car, to cross the street. Got in line next to a suited, bespectacled older gent. The short woman with brown hair and turquois dress to my left was recognizable as a slug veteran. Another gray-haired gent to her left and I joked about degrees of difficulty in egress and that penalties should be imposed on slugs not asking or pushing for the third rider (HOV 3 only requires two passengers and the driver). The suited gent and I got a two-door red Chevy GT with two attractive blonds already in the car. One got out to let us in, wearing black shorts and a T-shirt. When he got in, I joked to take his feet with him as they stuck under the front seat. Not much room in the back. The driver was a blond woman too. Young with white shorts and a loose T-shirt, slightly blue. Her rearview mirror was turned toward her as if she had been doing or checking her makeup. There was a sense of high energy in the car as well as cold, cold air conditioning. A scent of perfume or woman's deodorant or something filled the air. The two blonds giggled and spoke back and forth continuously. At one lurching stop, the driver apologized as another car cut in. WMZQ, country music again!

Three days straight. Winona Judd sang a funny-named song. News was budget bill passed by two votes, the Orioles beat Milwaukee 3–1, Ben McDonald winning his fifth straight. The gent read the paper briefly then put his head back to sleep. I dozed and looked out the window. The blond in back kept telling the blond driver what to do and where to go. They let me out at the light at the bottom of the off-ramp to the Pentagon. Wonder where they were going to work.

It had been dry for all of July and August until now. Today it began raining around 0800–0900 after arriving at work and tried to make up the rainfall deficit all in one day. Continuous heavy blowing rain. Hurricane Brett was forming up and aiming for the Caribbean, but our rain was independent of that storm. As I was walking to the slug line, my umbrella blew inside out several times, a small foldable pocket umbrella. It wasn't unusual after a storm like this the following day to see broken umbrellas lying in the gutters. Just discarded in disgust on the spot, I guess. Their carcasses littered the roads like so many dinosaurs now extinct. Good news was, with bad weather, the slug line was short, the fair-weather slugs taking alternative transportation, like buses or driving. Our driver was Sarge in short-sleeved shirt and baseball cap. Cold at first while we were wet. Then in traffic, the air conditioning was turned off. Traffic report on the radio was that all routes were delayed with multiple accidents. This is written while sitting still in HOV to public lanes at Springfield. Windows fogged repeatedly. Country western music, no talking.

Monday, 23 August 1993

After one week's vacation, another story. It was 0550, and I was in line next to a Marine in shorts with two bags. Tacky. Crossed the street with him and allowed him in ahead of me; it cost me as a Crystal City car pulled up and he and another guy got in. I worked up to first in line before the next Crystal City car pulled up. Recognized the driver as a former Navy officer. Guy in back and he talked awhile, then back seat resorted to a newspaper. WMZQ, country western station faded with traffic noise. It was just twilight as the driver took a Route 1 shortcut.

Master Chief Davidson going home. Halfway down HOV in general lanes, a small car was perpendicular to and squashed with a semi-tractor trailer's grill. A trickle of traffic was getting by, but the general impression was the flow of traffic stopped at the accident. It had just happened as no emergency vehicles were on the scene yet and people were running around.

Tuesday, 24 August 1993

Left the house at 0430 in order to gas up and arrive at the concrete factory in Crystal City in time to find a parking spot. Whenever free parking spaces become available in DC (the supply of parking), demand rushes to fill it. The result is all these cars with only the driver in them, usually napping until time to go to work. If you arrive late, you have to find a pay-to-park lot.

Wednesday, 25 August 1993

End of line at 0600 near Burger King. Who are all these people? At 0610, the Japanese lieutenant colonel in a Honda took three of us. One guy at the head of the line asking for Crystal City of each car. Luxury van. Stick shift stalled in front of the slugs. Started, lurched, stalled, started, laid rubber to the light, then stalled with a jerk to the slug line. We all looked at each other like, "Do we want to get in this van?" Obviously, an automatic driver with a stick shift van. Accident south of Belvoir slowed all traffic, normal and HOV, to the point we crossed the Occoquan Bridge at 0630. Not far in half an hour! We saw the two accident cars, police, tow truck, and flat bed.

Thursday, 26 August 1993

Twentieth in line. Air Force major again to my right. Older, rotund civilian to my left. Ninety-five degrees forecast with humidity so thick you could cut it with a knife. Buick LeSabre with a woman Navy commander with glasses driving. Plenty of leg room, Xtra oldies on the radio. Smooth riding, large car, no discussion. She was exceptionally cautionary in dropping me off at the light, preferring the parking lot, giving me extra steps to work.

Going home, Hal volunteered to give me a ride; his daughter showed up without the car, so we walked over to the Pentagon slug line. Got the two Marines in a red two-door sports car. They were in shorts and civilian clothes, air conditioning turned up to match the volume of rock music. I was deaf by the time we reached Tackett's Mill.

Friday, 27 August 1993

Hot moisture hung in the air. One hundred degrees with 95 percent humidity forecast. The slug line was short—I guess the oppressive weather was too much for the fair-weather slugs. But a civilian at the head of the line with a Crystal City sign was obnoxiously asking each car if it was going there. Then there was the two Army officers, a white lieutenant colonel and a black major who would only take one rider with room for two. I finally got a Toyota Corolla four-door car driven by a meek civilian guy with a mustache. Mystery man did not use any air conditioning or play the radio. And only drove 55 mph all the way in. Dangerous when all the HOV cars were doing sixty-five.

Monday, 30 August 1993

I got the last McDonald's side parking slot. Line stretched to the Burger King corner. Older gent to my right said, "This isn't too bad!" and then got out a handheld TV. News of Hurricane Emily could be heard as well as temperature eighty-five degrees and humidity 97 percent. After a short wait and several cars, a luxury van pulled up, and I was midline with the obnoxious guy at the end running forward. It was remarkable no one else was Crystal City bound. No air conditioning until on I-95 HOV lanes. Accident between Lorton and Newington. Driver didn't want to try the Route 1 alternative. As a result, we sat in heavy, heavy, heavy traffic. Which all could have been avoided. Fear of the unknown in taking another road he wasn't familiar with, I guess.

Tuesday, 31 August 1993

Long line again. Air Force was well represented in force. Line to second No Parking sign. Guy to right, civilian, had two bags and stayed right expecting quick movement, talking with a woman next to him. An Air Force captain behind me kept extra distance as if I had leprosy. Got an Olds '98 with a big woman with a short haircut. Guy in shotgun was small and like from the *American Gothic* painting. WTOP played while I dozed. No conversation. News was of NFL rosters and Hurricane Emily.

Wednesday, 1 September 1993

Arrived early at 0540. Still only about twentieth in line. Pleasant out, still clear, no effects from Hurricane Emily or a cold front. Saw Spitter in a nice short-sleeved shirt and colorful tie, looking fit. Got sixth in a van, the coffee-holding civilian clod ahead almost closed the door on me! Light strip down the left, air conditioning very cold, seat was very plush, a luxury van! Small short-haircut driver talked with the right-seat guy, an Army officer, who also got out when I did. No traffic issues.

Thursday, 2 September 1993

Second No Parking sign. Luxury van, cold, cold, cold. A meat locker. Guy asked for Crystal City, so I was deep selected. Popular music played as he took the KFC cutoff (Devil's Reach road), but light betrayed him. Unlike yesterday's van when the guy got a light to help the transition. It's a curious fact, as we discussed before, a median drop-off, the Pentagon people in a Crystal City car expect the Pentagon. Crystal City people in a Pentagon car get bottom of the hill at best. The driver, a smallish man with an abundance of hair, said he asked for Crystal City one morning and got one Pentagon guy that was surprised not to find himself at the Pentagon.

Going home. Short line. Got an oriental woman. Army officer and I got in back as she had a car seat in front right. As we got in, I thought, "Boy, it's hot. I can't wait until we get the air conditioning on." But it never came on and became painfully evident she didn't have it. Humidity over 95 percent, temperature over ninety, and every time we stopped, sweat broke out.

Friday, 3 September 1993

Labor Day before day; our car didn't start, and I had to move the car to keep the garbage truck off my back and hook up a charger. No problem at Tackett's Mill. As I suspected, traffic was light as government workers turned a three-day holiday into a four-day weekend. A big truck with the extended cab had trouble getting a third to sit behind the front seats and after several minutes left without a third. I got in rear left of a car; the woman to my right sat on the right. Two geeks with short haircut and glasses were in front. Driver was in the Army; right seat, a civilian. Around holidays, the natural slug order is disrupted. WMAL radio played, but they talked continuously. First, they repeated, "Pentagon, right?" to us. I said Crystal City, but I'll take bottom of the hill at the Pentagon. It was evident from their puzzled look they didn't know what I was talking about. I explained it. They then discussed Chicago (where I gathered the driver came from) and schools (Woodbridge Elementary). I learned the following while listening to them: The Kennedy Expressway has continual projects, a Cook County meeting discussed a new stadium, a new casino, or a new airport or more runways at O'Hare (in Chicago). Shotgun stated he liked fall—cool, fifty-degree weather, etc. And driver said, "Yes, except at football games in Chicago." They huddled around in groups with "warmers." A dome surely was thought of for Soldier Field. McCormick Place is next door, and the dome was to be called McDome!

Going home. I worked late and got to the slug line about 1600. About fifteen to twenty slugs ahead with slow pickups. Potomac Mills line was moving right along, pickups on both sides. One woman pulled up, asked for Potomac Mills, and no one moved. We in Tackett's Mill line shouted back, "Potomac Mills!" They said, "How many?" No answer. The woman was busy putting stuff in the trunk. I shouted, "Three!" to get the line moving. All the slugs laughed. It was hot and humid. Finally, I and another guy got a Cadillac SeVille. A red-haired guy was driving. He was with, it seemed, his wife, although she appeared older. The air conditioning was good, so that was a relief. The seats were plush, and the music classical. We were all set for the Labor Day commute! It only took an hour and a half to cover the usually half-hour trip, with all the traffic headed out on their holiday trips.

Wednesday, 8 September 1993

Dark, just after a brief shower. At second No Parking sign at 0545. Finally, a woman and I got a dark Hyundai two-door. The woman took back seat, and I took shotgun. Cold air conditioning directly on me, with a cold! Classical music played. Driver had dark, short hair, long sleeves, and a tie. Talked of government job cuts. He was in the military and the woman volunteered she worked in DC, with me working in Crystal City. Two cars fender bender in HOV north of Lorton delayed traffic, as did bridge work reducing four lanes to three.

Going home. More of Master Chief Davidson and his ice tea tanker.

Thursday, 9 September 1993

Hazy, misty, still dark. The McDonald's flagpole left a shadow shaft in the stores lights. At 0555, I was at the corner No Parking sign by Burger King! The line moved quickly until 0605. Then a lull. At 0610, three of us got picked up by a new Taurus. Short-haired business-like man at the wheel, with both hands. Soon he and the man behind him began a discussion that lasted the trip. I and the slug behind me didn't say a word. I couldn't doze for all the chitchat. Radio in the background. He took the left side, jumped right, and took Devil's Reach. A turning car was slightly over centerline, and he was reminded of a motorcycle incident he had. He was on a 90 cc bike, and a turning car didn't see him. Traffic in the wrong. He did a wheelie escaping. The back left rear guy was from New York and stuttered. He related an incident in his car that made no sense because he left out so much detail. The driver, however, egged him on by remembering roads and areas of Pennsylvania and New Jersey. They talked about the best routes *ad nauseum*. Then back to accidents. He had the requisite accident on I-95 when a van plowed into his old large clunker. She was more than sixty days in the area with no registration, etc. Divorced. They related the merits of four wheels over two. Truck blind spots (driver said) and accidents. New York said woman in a car was stuck under a tractor trailer. She escaped okay but didn't get into another car for six months. The truck driver was retired. I recalled the Ohio State trooper movie when I was in high school. When they interviewed the thirty-year veteran, he flatly stated he never had to unstrap a dead person. Strapping and/or belting in stuck with me to now.

Going home. Short line, about six people. Got a black Army sergeant that wanted to talk sports—Atlanta Braves two out of first place after being as much as eleven games behind in July. I said Orioles too. Car was a comfortable four-door sedan with three scented Christmas trees and a bag of pot, I would guess. The scent had long since left the trees. I felt I had ridden this car before as the instruments had white backgrounds, as though pasted on. Very unusual. Radio played, and I wrote this.

Friday, 10 September 1993

Thunderstorms last night. Ground was wet, but the overcast sky was clearing. Long line for a Friday! Air Force major to my left, me in right rear. A Navy captain (surface officer) rode shotgun, and the driver was a Coast Guard commander. The captain and commander talked continually. Big heads feeding big egos. The commander had just returned from Navy post graduate (PG) school and related all the base improvements to the captain. Soft jazz-rock played from the back speaker—yuck! The commander was playing the budget like the other services on cutbacks. Flew the Falcon jet and was going to Paris three days, Bordeaux two. "Better to deal with the manufacturer." After the commander's history and importance had been milked for all it was worth, the captain lit in with ship driving and PG school in '76. Somehow the conversation became lowered in volume and difficult to hear. As though the two were engaged in a secretive deal. Why weren't these guys discussing something important? Coasty then digressed into where all the bases were and how many planes.

Monday, 13 September 1993

Line was down to the second No Parking sign. Lined up next to a Navy captain I had ridden behind last Friday—he had a smirk on his face about something. I finally got a ride in a van. The captain sat on the left. No talking. Public radio news (PRN) of some kind. Then pop music. Driver was unsure of where to go, so we slugs provided it to him.

Going home. The line was halfway doubled back on itself. Hot but beautiful day. Twice a Dale City bus came and blew heat and exhaust on us. I and another guy got a pickup truck. Very uncomfortable. Scratchy music played. Guy to my right took up more than his share of room. My left leg was doubled back for the stick shift and transmission hump, fell asleep. I looked at Vermont ads while the guy slept.

Tuesday, 14 September 1993

Cool, nice, clear morning at 0540. Four of us got an extended caravan. WTOP news channel up front. The woman ahead took the jump seat, forcing me in back. PLO/Israeli treaty was news. Bears beat San Francisco in football.

Trip home was with an Army colonel. Slug line was one length long. Hot. Short woman in front of me was smoking and reading.

Wednesday, 15 September 1993

It was 0540. Short line, nice cool morning. Clear, stars still out. Two civilians in a new car asked for Crystal City. Deep selected! Long-sleeved driver with glasses. Not a word was spoken the entire trip. Radio played 107.3 FM: Carter, Ford, Bush, Clinton with Arafat. Car had both a temperature and time LED display. Arrived at 0620.

Going home. An Army captain was driving a Nissan four-door. Line was up to the bus stop shelter, about twenty- to thirty-minute wait. Car was hot at first, but he soon blew out the hot air for cool. You can tell where a car has been kept during the day—if cool in a parking garage, if hot in an outside lot. Two other slugs got in back. Easy commute, read from the Bible, Acts.

Thursday, 16 September 1993

Light drizzle at the second No Parking sign at 0545. Moved quickly. Short guy with a portable computer and umbrella to my left talked incessantly. I thought he was in one of the services but talked about how wonderful his company was. Older guy with long sideburns and glasses in a Cadillac DeVille picked up five of us. The Air Force officer ahead hesitated, so I jumped for the front right door. The talkative guy turned down the ride! Music from 96 FM Easy played on a crystal clear radio.

Soon after, these flyers were posted under our windshield wipers:

Public Notice

To: Commuters of Tackett's Mill Shopping Center
We appreciate your support and participation concerning our request to help alleviate the parking congestion at Tackett's Mill Shopping Center. However, there are still many commuters that are not adhering to the guidelines set forth by the center's ownership. Therefore, effective November 1, 1993 any vehicle parked at Tackett's Mill Shopping Center for more than three hours that is not located in the designated commuter lot will be towed at owner's expense.

This was part of the recognition at both ends that the commute slugging was not going to go away. By October 1994, I was commuting from a different slug line at a new shopping center, Dillingham Square, across from our subdivision, but that's another story, part of over thirty years commuting to Washington, DC.

ABOUT THE AUTHOR

Kerry Young and his family—Susan, Colleen, and Christian—moved to Lakeridge, Virginia, in October 1985. For twenty-two years, he commuted to Washington, DC, to his DOD contractor support job at both the Naval Air and Sea Systems Commands. Reducing commuting cost and time was a common goal for thousands of government and contractor workers then and now. He retired from the Navy after twenty years flying helicopters from ships on five deployments with over four thousand flight hours. One more child was born before retiring, Megan. Commuting efficiency played a role in supporting all three kids' activities, from swim meets to hockey to dance lessons. Just like thousands of other daily DC commuters.

www.ingramcontent.com/pod-product-compliance
Lightning Source LLC
Chambersburg PA
CBHW021138260726
48656CB00023B/327